LIFE ADVENTURES

LIFE ADVENTURES

LAUREN "BUZZ" YODER

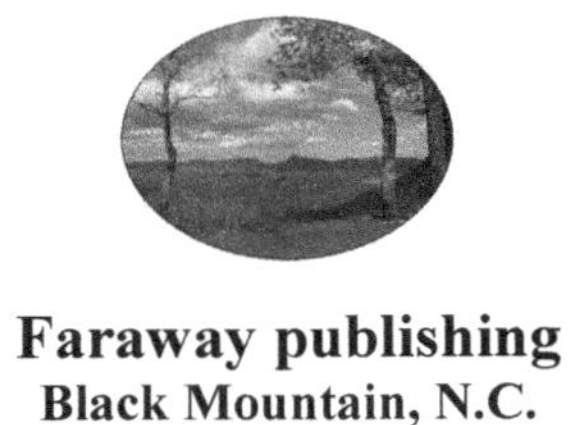

Faraway publishing
Black Mountain, N.C.

The author may be contacted at
41 Wagon Trail
Givens Highland Farms
200 Tabernacle Road
Black Mountain, NC 28711
laurenw.yoder@gmail.com

Published by
FARAWAY PUBLISHING
125 Spring View Drive
Black Mountain, N.C. 28711
farawaypublishing@gmail.com

ISBN-13: 979-8-9881761-5-2 (pbk.)
Library of Congress Control Number: 2024935306

Printed in the United States of America
10 9 8 7 6 5 4 3 2 1

Cover photograph
Le Canal du Midi, by Lauren Yoder
Cover Design by Brian Wilson
All photographs by Lauren Yoder,
except Sydney Wilson's watercolor
of La Grange de Meslay, in Meslay, FR

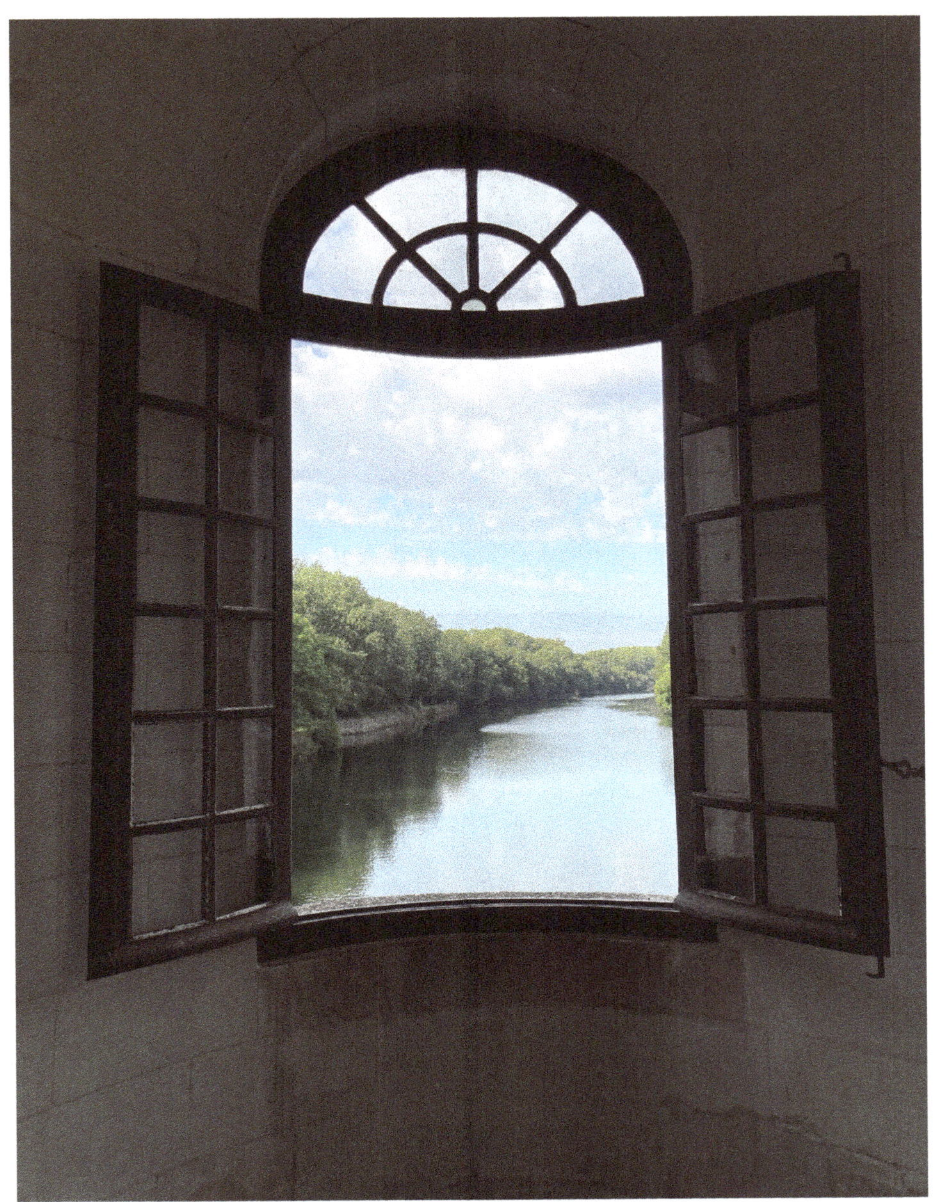

V

CONTENTS

ILLUSTRATIONS

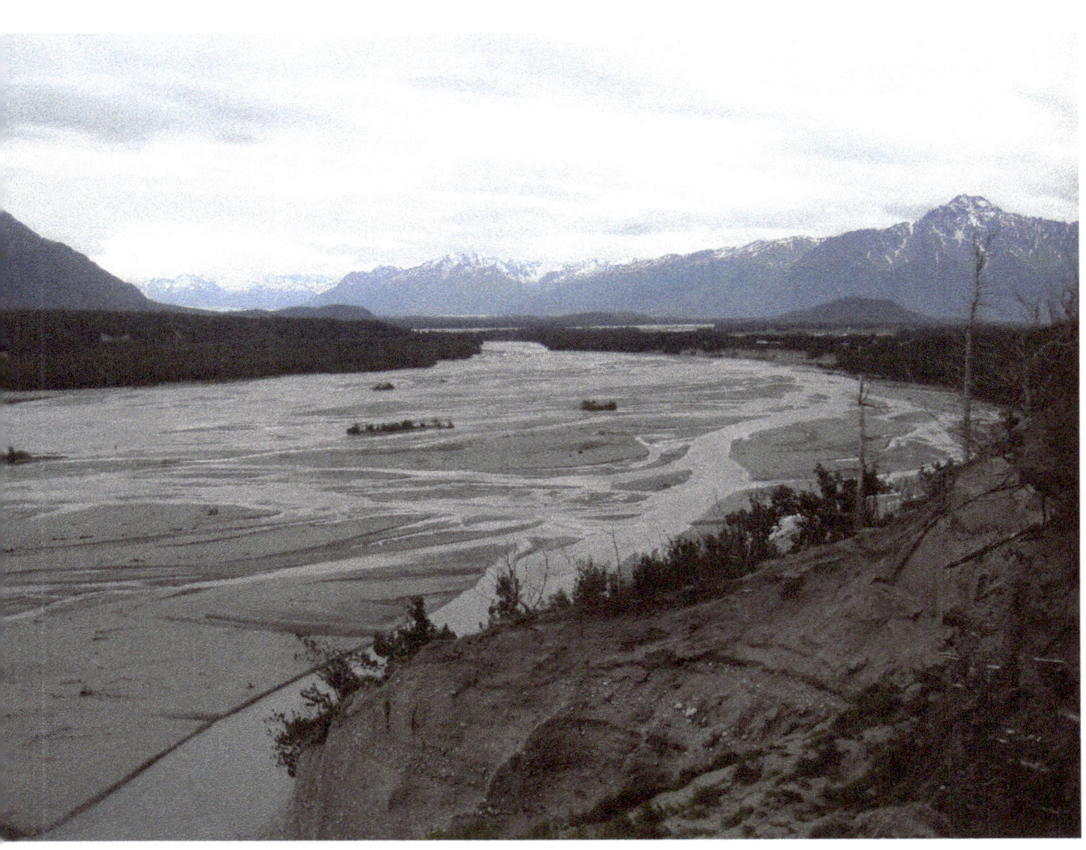

Over the years, in France, in Africa, and here at home, I have often sat down to play with words. There may be some personal experience or news event that triggers the compulsion to put pen to paper. And I typically find my inspiration in nature or from places that have been significant in my life. Some can be seen as love poems. I am grateful to Sydney, who with her layout skills first gathered together and formatted a representative selection of my efforts for my 80th birthday!

Acknowledgments

I have many people to thank for their contributions to a life enriched by books, travel, and friendships. First of all my parents, Lauren and Nina Yoder, who loved to read about far-off places and instilled in me a thirst for the wonders of the world, both natural and man-made. My late wife, Suzanne, shared my experiences in France, Africa, and Latin America. She was my joyful partner in our volunteer positions in national parks and forests, and wherever we were, she always encouraged me to jot down my impressions.

I would like to dedicate this collection in loving memory to my daughter, Jocelyn, who brought me and others joy for fifty years before her life was cut short too early, and to honor my son, Reinald, and his wife Christine, who share my love of food and of exploring new geographies and cultures.

I also thank my poetry friends in Black Mountain, North Carolina, who were often the first to listen patiently to many of my poems and who graciously accepted them. The decision to use my photographs was made easier by my friends in our photo club, who helped me develop my skills, mostly with a simple smartphone camera.

I would especially like to acknowledge the beauty and the serenity that my supportive wife, Sydney Wilson, has brought to my life with her eye for color, form, and texture. Our competitive spirits require that when she creates a lovely art piece, I am compelled to compose a poem, and vice versa.

Without the patience and the professional help of my editor and publisher, Ran Shaffner, this collection of poetry would never have seen the light of day, and for that I thank him.

Winter Haikus, 2023

On this new morning
The clouds awaken crimson,
Warning all sailors.   Jan 11

I walk in drizzle.
The mountains display blue tints
Sheltering us all.   Jan 17

Rain splashes on pond,
Creates concentric circles.
Are the fish watching?   Jan 19

Gray skies hang above.
Wet tears course slowly downward,
Chilling waiting earth.   Jan 25

North wind quiets down.
The freezing temperature
Forms icy patterns.   Feb 4

Just before sunrise
Full moon suspended in West,
Carrying my dreams.   Feb 6

The wren's cheery notes
And bluebirds' liquid chirping
Waken heart's warm song.   Mar 2

On far mountain ridge
Tall winter oak trees stand bare,
Patiently waiting.   Mar 4

Cold wind brings in rain
Lashing yellow daffodils.
Can thin stalks stay strong?   Mar 7

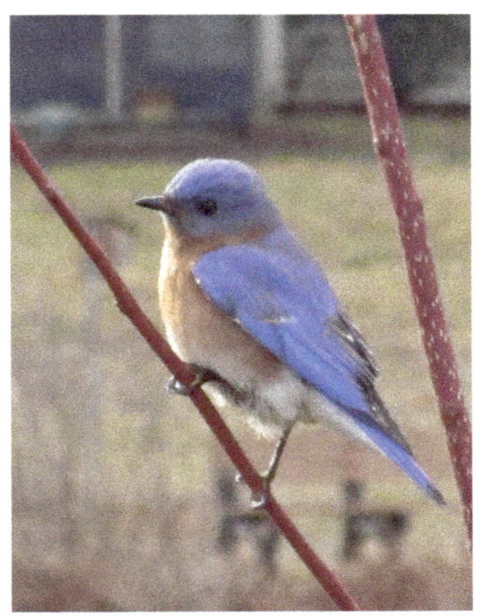

Messenger of Peace

Each morning, oft before dawn's fingers rise to greet,
My good retriever, golden in starlight, nudges me awake.
She pushes screen door open,
And we step out together,
She bounding down the steps and me scanning the eastern sky
In April, fondly noting Jupiter rising near the morning star
Or rusty Mars and ringed Saturn high above the horizon.
She, in season, seeks out Sirius, the dog star,
Faithfully following Orion his own master.

But this morning she can only drag herself along,
Whimpering slightly and panting.
I half lift her back up the steps,
And she collapses on the porch
Near the sheltering white oak tree.
I caress her trembling head and sit quietly in prayer.
As the night greys and turns to day,
The planets fade and new grey-green oak leaves stand out against pale sky.

Never has a white-breasted nuthatch graced my yard,
But this morning as I stroke my old retriever's golden coat,
A visiting nuthatch creeps headfirst down oak trunk,
Black-white feathers and razor-sharp beak silhouetted against brown bark.
With raised head, her white throat flashes in the morning light.
She drops down to porch deck,
Cocks her head,
Circles round my canine friend,
Then, almost unbelievably,
Hops up on her back,
Angelic bringer of tranquility.

My dear friend struggles to lift her head,
Looks at the comforting messenger nuthatch,
Raises her eyes to me,
Mine wet with tears,
Then drops her head
And drifts into never-ending peace,
As the nuthatch flies off to other tasks, leaving me in grief
But in awesome wonder at nature's loving gifts.

Tea Room on a Rainy Day

Drizzle in the street
Chilling our bones.
Behind the vitrine in Vitry
Beckon chocolate éclairs,
Apricot tarts,
Little fruit pastries,
Blackberries,
Red cherries,
Crimson currants
Glowing through sugar glaze,
Waiting to accompany
Hot green tea.

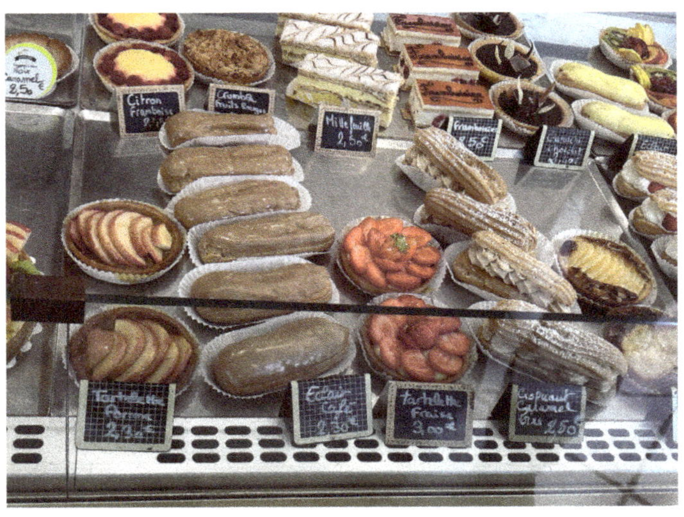

Truffle Dog

Fifteen years ago I planted truffle oaks,
roots enriched with fungal spores.
As I dug each hole to embrace those roots,
you, too, Cachou, then just a pup,
dug furiously with forepaws,
tossing russet earth and pebbles.

As I carried water
from the nearby river,
you gamboled by my side,
bumping the bucket
and lapping muddy water,
as I soaked each tree.

For five years we waited,
you faithfully by my side,
wondering why each week
I returned to watch
my grove of oaks
inching oh so slowly skyward.

Then one December day
you ran ahead
and stopped beside a tree,
not unlike its neighbors.

You sniffed the air,
looked up at me,
put your nose to the bare earth,
and began to scratch.

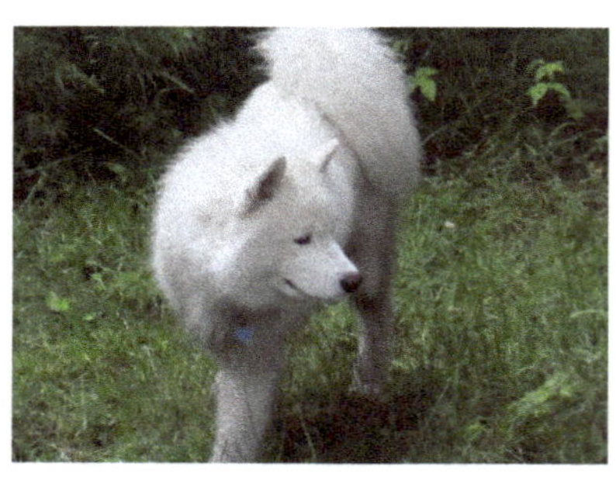

You pulled the soil away,
laying bare black lumps on roots,
round and soft,
the size of bantam eggs,
aroma wafting on the breeze.

I knelt down
with great care as you watched,
nose quivering,
and with my knife, my trusty Opinel,
I lifted truffles to my nose,
wondrous culinary treats.

4

Each year since, a whole decade,
as winter winds defoliate my truffle oaks,
you've run from tree to tree,
drawn by black diamond fragrance.

Today, fifteen years have passed
since as a pup you pranced and frolicked.
Each night you've slept at my bed's foot,
each morning greeting me bright-eyed.

But now your eyes are weak,
and forelegs no longer dig,
you lie silently by water bowl,
telling me it's time to go.

I carve small bits of last year's truffle,
fold them into omelette, as if for me myself.
You look up weakly, lick the bowl
for one last taste.

You close your eyes,
and I can sense a canine smile;
then, my faithful truffle dog
drifts off, leaving me alone.

Grey Catbird

Balanced by long black tail,
the catbird extends his beak,
carefully plucking plump blueberry,
still slightly pink like rabbit's eye.
He stares in the window
and winks, knowing
that berry will never fully ripen
and with its sweet acidity
enhance my breakfast bowl.

Lascaux Animal Spirits

I grind to powder charcoal
and clay ochres, red and yellow,
then mix with water to make a paste.
I slip into the sacred cave,
as did the ancient ones.
Standing on a narrow ledge,
I whisper to the spirit of the black bull,
the totem of my family.

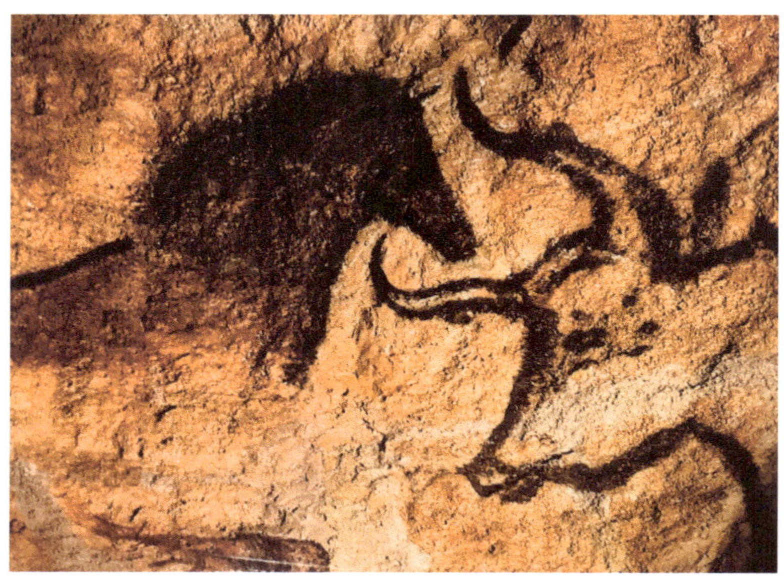

In the thick darkness,
I feel the living, breathing earth
through subterranean shafts
and sense the shadowy spirits of
horses, bears, and bison
watching from above and from years past.
Holding high my flickering wick
of oil-filled torch, I scan the hallowed walls.

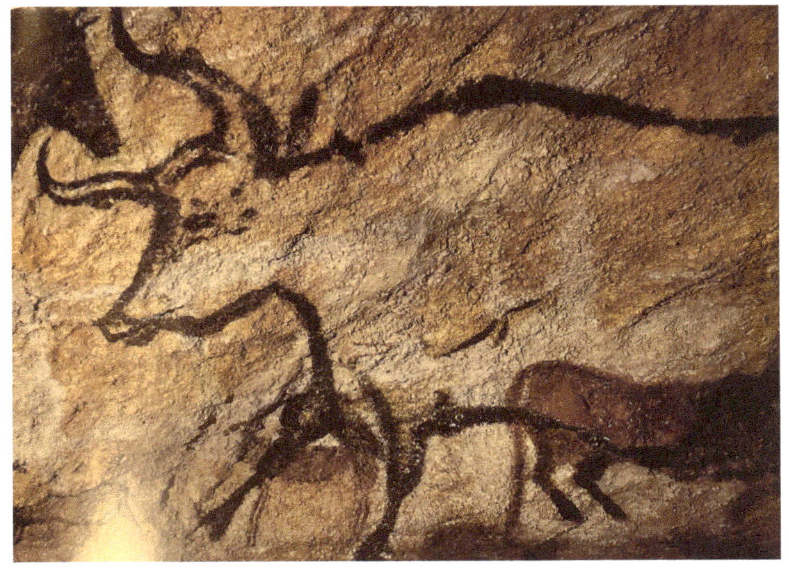

I dip into my bull-horn cups
with frayed oak branch
or rolled skin swabs
and, near russet stags and yellow horses
painted on these rock walls
through countless generations,
I find the space
to dab with care the colored pigments,
red, black, and yellow.

And with these colors, especially black,
an aurochs bull takes shape
and begins to breath and paw the ground.
I raise a hymn to animal spirits,
a song of praise for artistry,
lauding creation,
bringing game
within the arc of spear,
and linking past with present.

Daffodils and Sunflowers

Here in evening's clear late winter sky,
we spy the tiny crescent moon,
newly reappeared
and poised in nightly rise toward Orion
and faithful Dog Star Sirius.
Our geese lift noisily from the darkened pond,
seeking shelter in parts unknown.
Daffodils have sprouted golden,
as have crocuses, purple, white.
All is quiet as we walk,
save the rustling wind through budding maple trees,
peepers joining springtime chorus,
and in the distance, planning nightly tryst,
a pair of screech owls.

Meanwhile, in a country to the east,
where sunflowers once waved tall in fields,
there too the moon is waxing crescent
and faithful Sirius there still follows
his hunter-master high in winter's nighttime sky.
But instead of golden moonlit daffodils,
red tracers streak from deadly booms.
Replacing avian song and choral peepers,
explosions lift their darkling smoke,
obscuring heavens and hope,
beckoning not loving owls
but ravenous black kites and swooping vultures.

There brothers stare down rolling tanks,
in darkened stairwells children whimper,
some loved ones, uprooted,
seek safety on the frozen roads,
uncertainty awaiting
after border crossings.
What welcome there awaits?
And will they see abandoned homes again?

In gratitude I love my crescent moon
and cherish moonlit daffodils,
breathe in my fresh and peaceful mountain air
unspoiled by smoke and hate.
But when, tonight, a continent away,
lungs choked by dust and grime,
my brothers face the barrel of a gun
and sisters weep as children's futures splinter,
may I not neglect to look for paths of solidarity,
to seek to foster furtive justice here,
to hope that sunflowers will in every land
raise golden faces to the light.

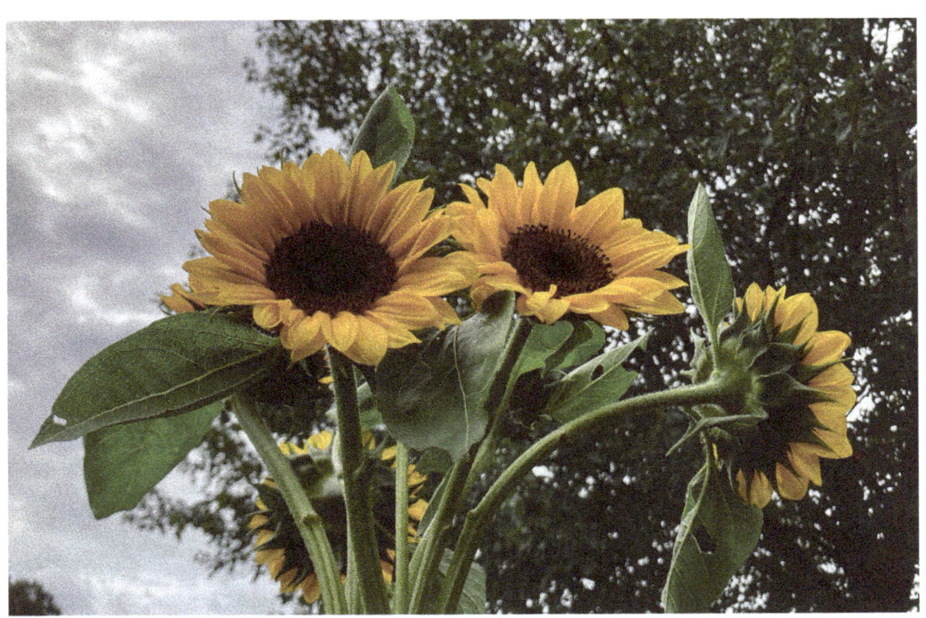

Reservation Boarding School

For breakfast my mamma would bring corn and pumpkin,
Spiced with chiles and tomatillos;
In the red cliffs above our home,
Nested the masters of the wind, golden eagles
And swift-diving peregrine falcons.
The blue sky shimmered in the noonday sun,
And our little garden thirstily drank
From a dripping spring,
Giving life to burgeoning pumpkin shoots
And green corn stalks waving in the breeze.
I watched my daddy chant his morning prayers,
Facing east at sunrise, turquoise stone in hand,
Keeping faith with clan tradition,
Speaking sacred words in our ancestral tongue,
Bringing us all into harmony with land and sky
And with the source of all being.
My grandpa, nearly blind,
Helped me choose a small, straight cedar branch,
Richly red and aromatic, and with a small hand drill
Bored his love of music into its hollowed core,
His obsidian knife cutting clean even holes
Into my new flute, my breath and fingertips
Linking me to the songs of the meadowlark
And other sacred wind-whispering tunes.

Then rode up a tall white man in uniform.
"Bureau of Indian Affairs," the badge proclaimed.
His orders placed me in a cart,
and we set off for the boarding school,
where now, my sixth birthday past,
I would live and learn to be civilized.
I tightly clasped my leather bag.
Inside were links to home and history:
Seven grains of purple corn,
A hallowed turquoise pebble,
And ancestral songs nestled in my cedar-perfumed flute.

When the door slammed shut behind me,
They dressed me in white shirt and navy shorts,
Forbidding my sacred mother tongue.
They tossed my blue corn kernels,
They crushed my turquoise stone,
They broke my song-filled flute.

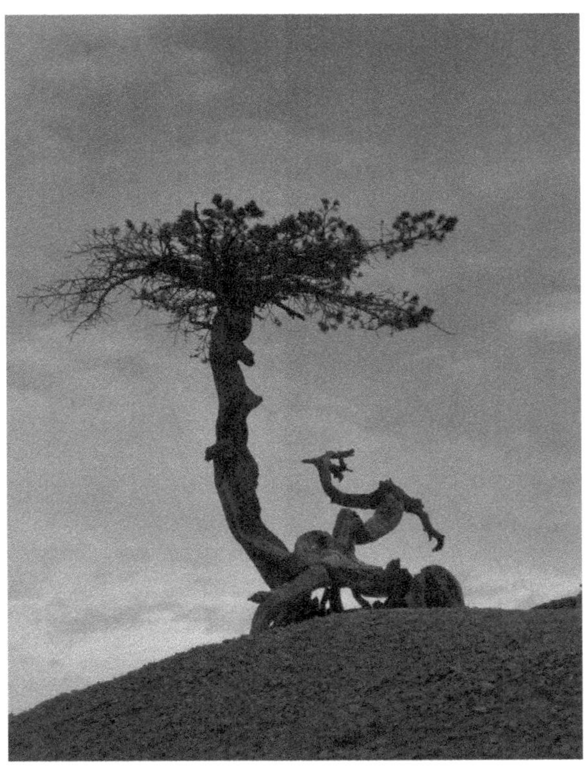

Crumbling

As social structures crumble around us,
and invisible dangers lurk,
may I remember the beauty of moments past,
of human warmth and love
that brighten days and comfort nights,
of ordinary joys
so rich with meanings,
of risks taken
and rewards that followed.

A daily morning walk
with chirping daughter
on the way
to school and office,
with bluebirds' liquid twittering
in party lines
from wires above.

With teenage friends
in camaraderie
on hot Saturday afternoons,
lolling on a sandbar
and diving deep to cool water
in the tidal channel,
escaping biting horseflies.

Lying in my back
on August nights,
slapping mosquitoes,
counting meteoric flashes
in the star-strewn arching dome
along with Perseus
and the beloved,
wondering at the marvels
of our expanding universe
and deepening love.

At a sidewalk café in Brussels,
with a monastery brew
and open journal pages
awaiting scratch of fountain pen,
transcribing novel tastes
of potatoes fried in donkey grease,
drenched with mayonnaise,
and served in newsprint cones.

With students,
ebony faces glistening in the firelight,
listening to animal tales,
and sharing riddles,
eager to face the future,
though in a deserted mission village
half-destroyed by
heartless rebels
powered by both greed and fear.
Paddling together
toward Blueberry Island,
souls and senses in perfect harmony
on remote Alaskan lake,
loons calling through the fog
and cow moose splashing off the island,
impervious to our insignificance.

And now, in awesome spring,
as in our Carolina mountains,
early season flowers awaken—
toothwort, lily, and painted trillium—
though calamity threatens on every side
and expectations crumble,
we can bask together
in the beauteous blossoms
and burgeoning bonds.

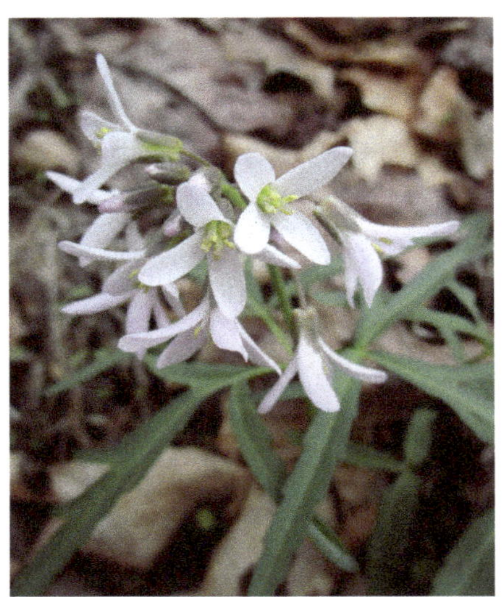
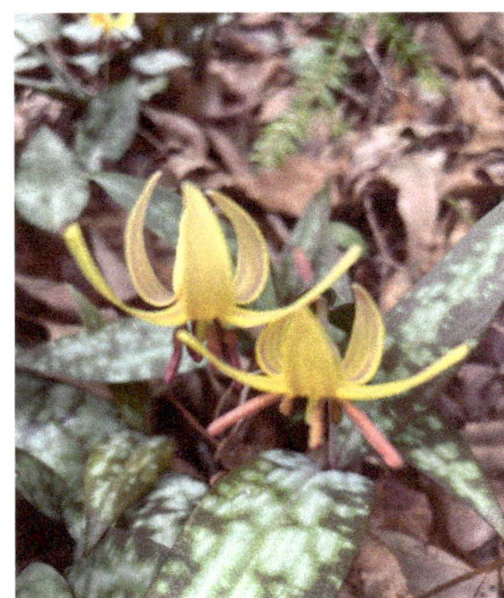

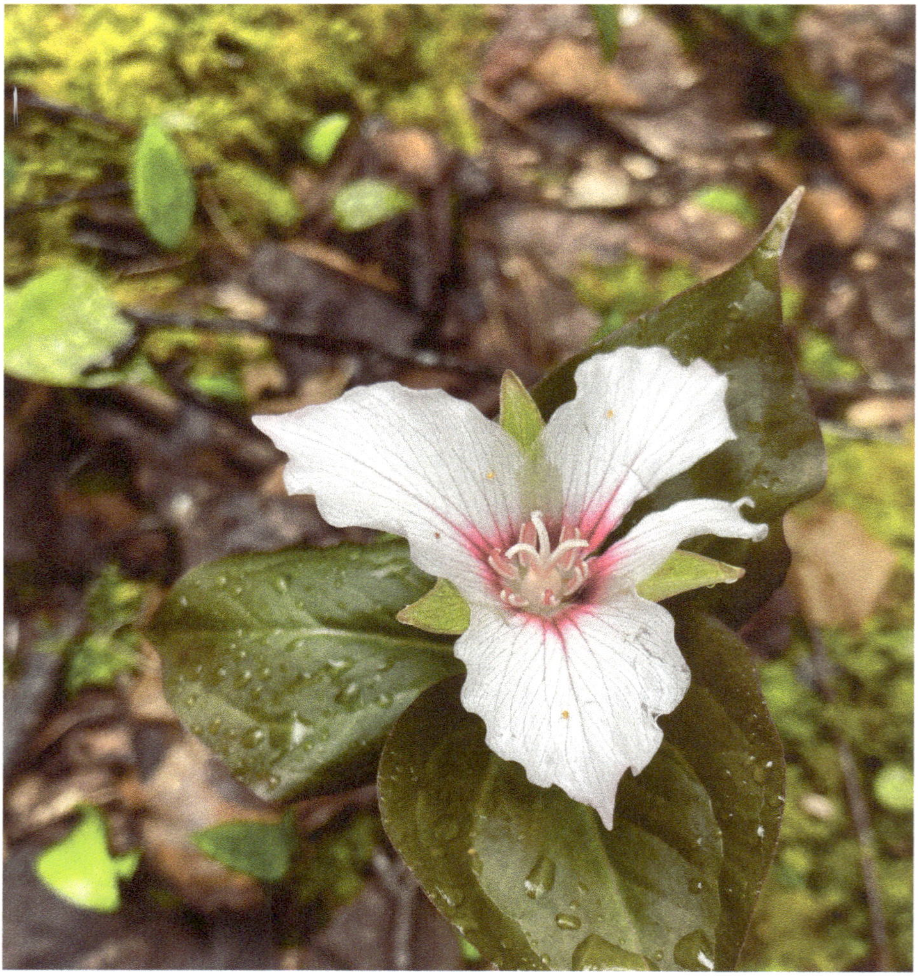

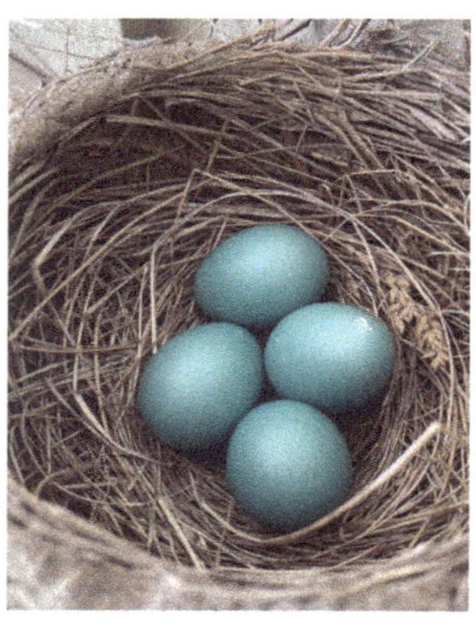

Four Eggs

Four eggs,
Brown speckled,
No higher than a fox's nose:
Life snuffed ere it begins?
Beaks ajar
When mother flies in.
Then fledglings rise:
Fox foiled for now.

Earth Surgery

Red jaws open wide
smash epidermic concrete walls
rip earth asunder
ancient culverts pulled like bones
tendons of pipes and wires
opening springs of water that runs like blood.
Mother Earth invaded, ravaged,
scraps of metal like petrified wood
useless body parts
stacked together to be discarded
red clay hangs from bare roots
that stretch forlornly toward the sky.
Painful surgery.

ER portal swings open wide
to workers with yellow vests,
swarming like termites
stretching lines for sutures
firm foundations laid
bandaging torn earth
plaster casts for shattered bones
transfusion pipes aligned
rebar as hip replacement platinum
awakens dreams of pain-free living
and hope regained.
New walls arise
future shelter for communal joy
fine dining, stage events, and music.
Sweet recovery.

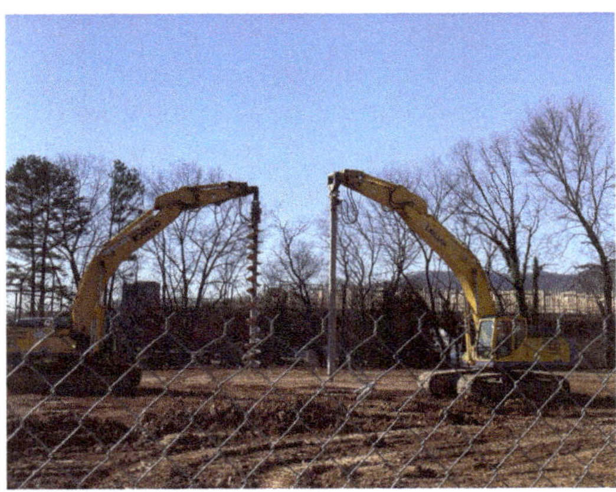

When Our Earth Flattens

This morning's news reports
one more conspiracy afoot.
That grand conspiracy
by scientists and priests
has hid for centuries
what true believers know:
that Terra Firma's truly flat.

Those true believers also see
that laws of Science are mere inventions
to hide the truth.
Vaccinations harm not help,
moon walks are but a prank,
climate change is naught but fantasy,
and of course facts are fiction,
and mainstream media is never to be trusted.

Where do we turn
when life seems meaningless,
when truth is only relative,
when hate and meanness thrive,
when floods rise and fires rage,
when, as Auden says,
"Things fall apart; the centre cannot hold,"
or when Maya Angelou describes us as
"this people on this mote of matter
in whose mouths abide cankerous words"?

Where might we find our solace?
Where might appear the stable centre
that always truly holds?

We first give thanks for Nature's marvels.
Consider the hummingbird's iridescent plumes
and her beating wings we cannot see.
Consider how trees speak to neighbors
through fungal networks entwined with roots.
Remember the broad expanse of Milky Way
as brilliance fades with rising harvest moon.
And note the intricacy: the emerald seeds
of orange jewelweed
that pop when touched.

And too we cherish created worlds
and feelings that poets bring to life.
The sonority of individual language
that touches chords divine within our soul,
the creation of images
juxtaposed in novel ways,
musical words
awakening deeply buried memories,
links with history,
and sounds from other shores.

But most of all,
our solace and deep meaning,
our courage and our strength,
come from fellow creatures.
Those newly met in hospitals,
whose healing hand and tender words
cure not pain and malady alone
but restore as well our faith in love.
And what better recipe for
returning to the centre
than a friend's warm smile,
a strong embrace,
or even an emoji's grin.

So, as for me,
when things seem to fall apart
around me,
no flat earth theory.
I opt for directing eyes
to rippling river and spruce-green forest,
preparing ears
for the beauty and melody of words,
and opening heart
to the warming rays of friendship!

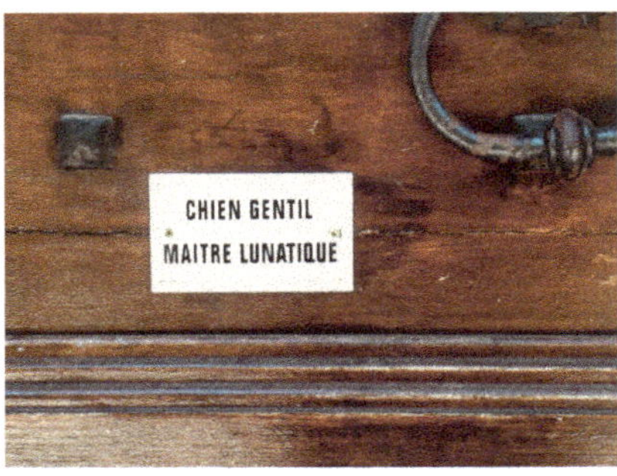

Black-faced Sheep

Black-faced sheep
Grazing downhill
In thick green grass.
Sheep that Joan from Arc
Guided home one night
In 1412 after her visions.
"I will lead my army
Against the English
Like I lead my sheep!"
Over the hill came
Not English lancers
But wolves from the woods.
But Joan was already
Heading southwest
On her way to Chinon
To meet Charles.

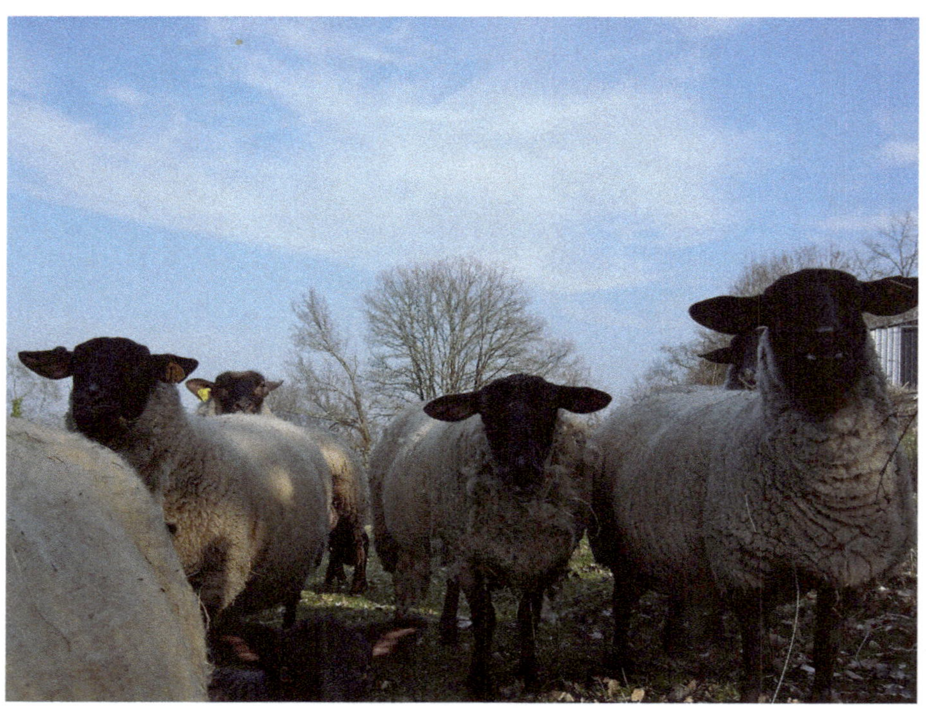

Le Lac des Corbeaux

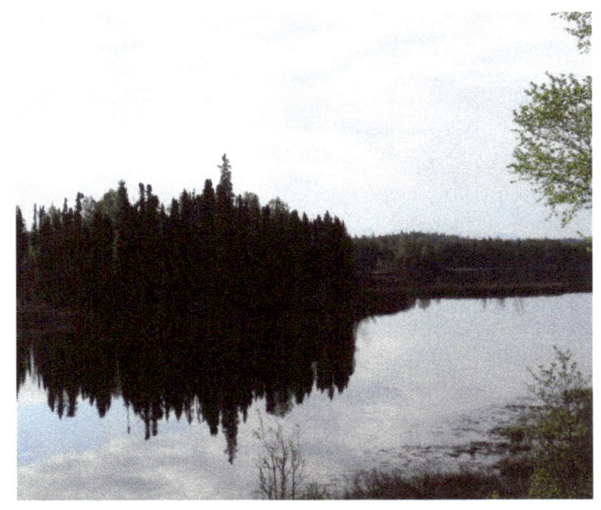

Lake of the Crows,
Nearby as the crow flies
But distant by the twisting road
With no room to pass.
Brown goats in the steep meadow,
Source of Cabriolet,
Tasty goat cheese.
Green water reflecting
Deeper green forests
And on gray-green moss-covered rocks
A noon meal—
Shredded red cabbage,
Couscous with bits of mint,
Crimson-glazed raspberry tart
With rich brown Carte Noire coffee.

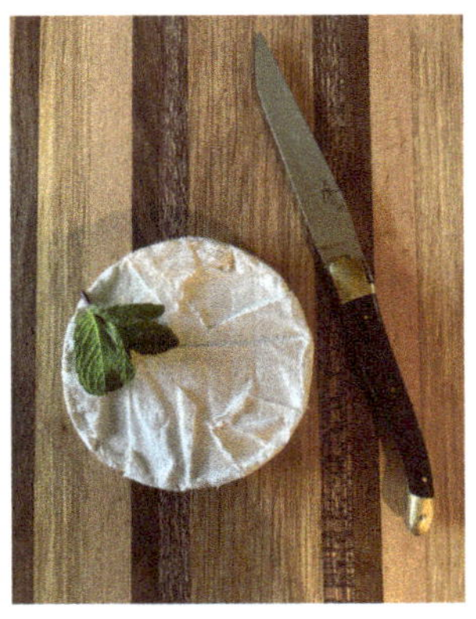

The Observer

Through your eyes
I learned to watch the world.
Sparkling and alert,
they let nothing slip by unseen,
unexamined,
and unappreciated.

Human gestures,
perhaps tightly crossed arms
or sheepish smiles,
turned down mouths
or wrinkled brows—
all conveyed to you
deeply set emotions
and gave you insight
into fellow souls.

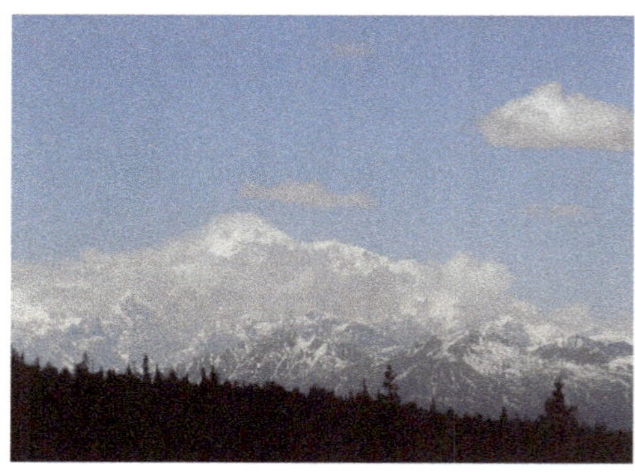

You admired
those who dressed with flair,
not fancy or extravagant
but simply and attractively.
"A flower," you said
"shares simple form and color."
"The iridescent hues
of hummingbirds
add loveliness to the world we love."
And so you of yourself took care
with touch of color,
a scarf, a hat,
and vests with pockets,
adding simple flair, like flower or bird.

You spent many an evening,
me immobile by your side,
our chairs by Gem Creek,
watching beavers
gnaw through willow trunks,
repair their dam,
or simply cavort in water games.

What delight
when you discovered
a beaver skull
and two long front teeth
to store with other finds,
bird eggs, sharks teeth,
in a shoe box,
your museum,
to show to grandchildren!

Or on our balcony,
overlooking Lake Tanganyika,
you marveled as you watched
the sky darken
with the wondrous daily migration
of fruit bats,
thousands, perhaps millions,
leaving for their nightly trip
to the distant forest
in search of sustenance.

You found delight
in nature's simple scenes—
a phoebe hawking,
then carrying the insect
to its nest;
two billygoats
butting heads;
a rainstorm sweeping
across the Rio Grande valley;
the full moon rising
through winter's poplar trees;
yellow evening primrose,
blossoms slowly unfurling
at dusk
by Lake Tomahawk;
heart-shaped Galax leaves
on mountain trails,
turning red
for Valentine's Day.
Sometimes you tweaked nature
to better observe its marvels.

Remember the day
you carried a dead raccoon,
road kill,
to our backyard,
attracting a wake of feeding vultures—
a living tableau
for our family Thanksgiving dinner?

You often joked
that you should have become
a naturalist,
living with gorillas in Rwandan mists
or chimps in the green hills of Burundi.
But what a marvelous
observer you would have been,
curious, admiring,
meticulous, persistent,
and above all,
loving and respecting God's creatures,
giving thanks for nature
and the beauty of our earth.

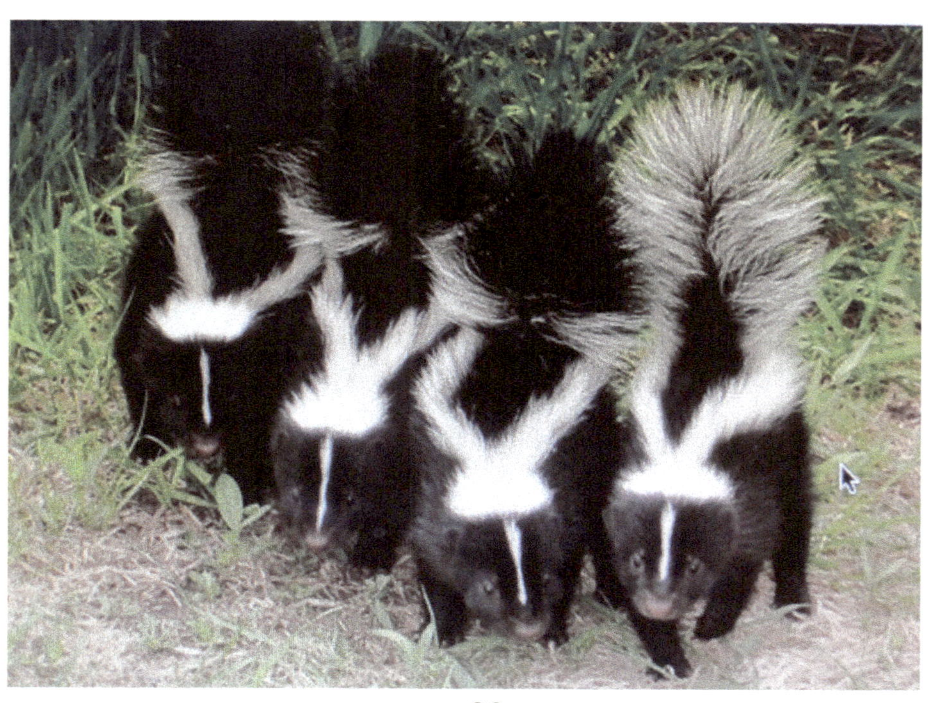

Assateague Light

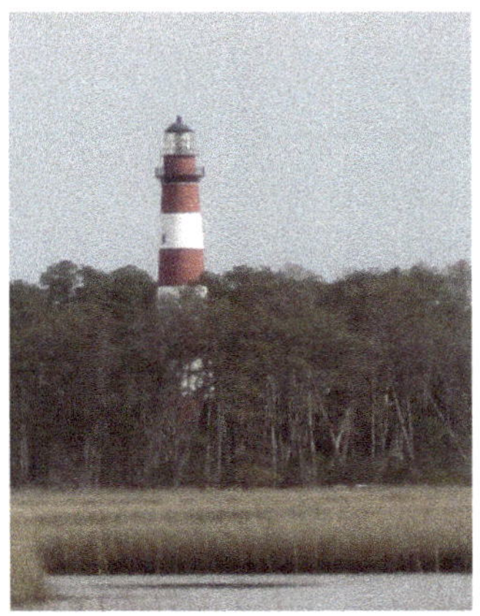

Watchful,
like the lighthouse,
rust-red, your favorite color,
and purest white,
reaching above
tall loblolly pines,
waving marsh grass,
and a solitary heron.

The light in your eyes
shines upon
those you cherish,
guiding
the wayward to safety—
an inspiration
to those who pick up litter
along your shores
and pathways,
providing
assurance to all.

As the island migrates
through life's nor'easters,
on Misty fall mornings,
and under dark thunderclouds,
you stand firm,
unshakable,
a beacon of hope,
my guiding light.

Our Rivers

Rivers sprung from your gardens of Eden,
not Tigris and Euphrates,
but Kwilu, Loire,
Ruzizi, and Swannanoa.

Rivers constantly moving,
cleansing the land,
bringing nutrients to the soil,
flowing to the sea,
carrying away our concerns,
blending our experiences,
in flood or in drought—
symbols of the passage of time.

You could sit for hours
by their banks,
watching beavers in Gem Creek,
admiring herons wading,
using a long stick
to fish out detritus.

You called out danger to tourists
venturing dangerously close
to hippos,
pitied the migrating wildebeests
dragged under by waiting crocs
as they crossed the Mara.

Post-genocide reports of bodies
choking the Akagera
turned you for a time away from rivers,
from their beauty,
from the peacefulness.

And you longed
for a log cabin
hidden in the hemlocks
far from town
along the purity
of a mountain stream.

You kept a cloth-covered notebook,
now a gift to me,
with a theme of rivers,
complete with poems,
quotations,
personal thoughts,
pictures of our picnics.
Thus you shared
your love of nature,
your gift of observation,
your eye for beauty,
your desire for peace.

And your constant advice
to me was
"Go with the flow!"

Great Blue

Come down to the pond with me.
Let us learn from the heron
carried in on wide-swept wings
flashing blue and gray
in the morning sunlight.
He now stands patiently near the bank,
head poised for a strike,
confident in his skill,
like a fisherman
who knows he can fill his creel.

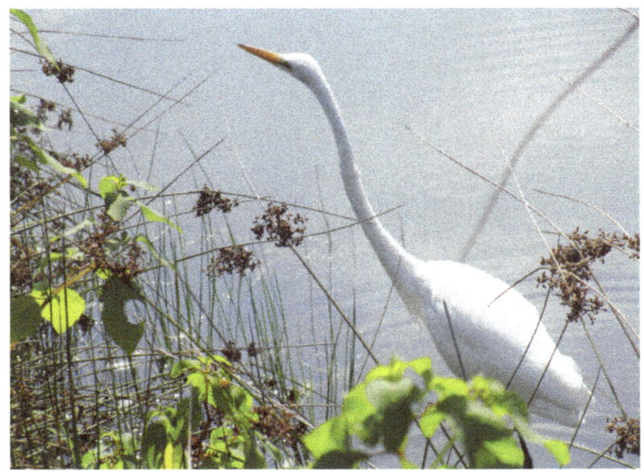

The Cardinal Flower

As long, hot days begin their transformation
to cooler nights and early morning fogs,
the cardinal flower, near gurgling creeks
and rippling ponds,
again waves scarlet flags on deep green stems,
like the fireweed we loved,
blossoms moving up its sturdy stalks
along Alaska's lakes and streams,
announcing summer's end.
Harbingers of cold, of loneliness,
of gathering darkness and of grief,
a symbol of the end.
But reminders too of longer days,
of warmth, of green vigor,
of joyous smiles,
of shared experiences,
like light, water, and oxygen
in photosynthesis,
producing energy
and nourishment for growth
and hope-filled future life.
In late summer of that fateful year,
we left high desert flowers,
barrel cactus and Indian paintbrush,
newly blown with monsoon rains,
returning to our mountain home
weighted down with knowledge
of our own near end.
Twice, as body weakened,
once in friend's convertible,
with blue sky above
but dark clouds massed on the horizon,
you asked to see your favorite flowers,
where faithfully in prior years
they stood foretelling change of seasons,
the beauty of sourwood leaves
and the silence of falling snow.

Again, today, I stand
in reverence, hat removed,
tear in eye, but smile on face,
in awe before the floral joy
of deep-red cardinal,
standing tall in cassock,
blessing all creation.
Harbinger of disappearance, yes,
and loneliness.
But also symbol of created
memories, of light, of warmth,
of love so deeply shared.

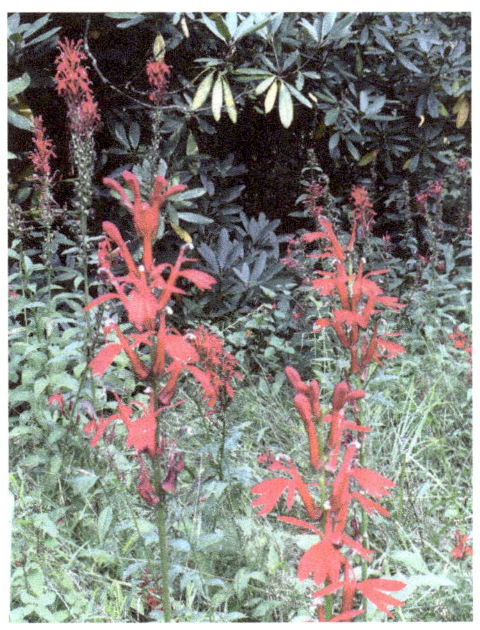

Mountain Cider

Screech went the crank of the old cider mill;
his gnarled hands, still strong,
grasped the rusty red handle.
Into the wide bin above
I tossed apples, some red, some yellow,
gathered from across the mountain road
from under twisted ancient apple trees
planted by his grandfather.

"When he plowed this holler with a mule,
a hundert years ago," he said,
giving the handle a few more cranks.
"Now my neighbors use gas engines
to make their cider.
But grandpa's tasted better,
and this here mill was his."

The screeching crank kept turning,
and streams of amber juice gushed out,
a feast for wasps and yellow jackets.
"Here," he said, handing me a tin cup
filled with the frothy ambrosia.
"Like my grandpa gave me."

I brushed away two buzzing yellow jackets
and brought the cup to lip.
Slightly sour but oh so warm and sweet,
opening images of the holler long ago
and an old mountain man
passing along a cup of love.

Mushroom Limericks

Whenever we go for a walk,
There are always mushrooms to stalk.
But as much as I scuffle,
I never hear truffles.
If only all fungi could talk!
On our hikes I keep scanning the ground
To see which good 'shrooms can be found.
In looking for flavor,
I find little to savor,
But colors and textures abound.
And mostly because I'm in haste,
It's hard to find mushrooms to taste.
Too rarely chanterelles,
Almost never morels,
So often I come back shamefaced!
A mycologist's word to the wise:
"Be mindful of beauty and size.
To avoid being dead,
Please use your head,
And avoid Death Angel's surprise!"

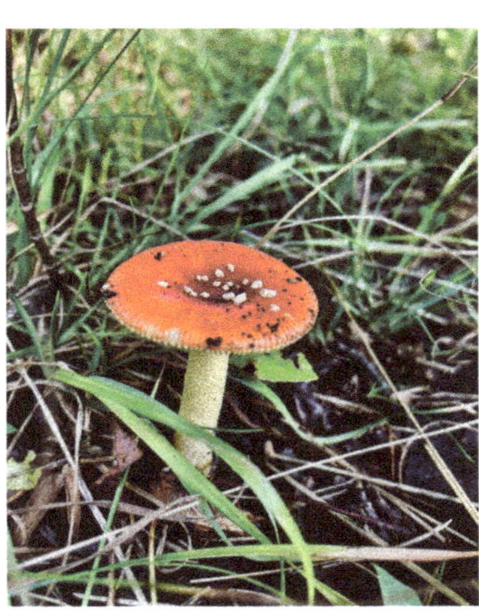

Nettles, Berries, Grapes

In my early springtime garden,
beds of stinging nettles thrive
and raise great welts on fingers bare.
But clipped with care,
they soon become a tasty soup,
so creamy, green, and luscious.
My berry canes in hot July,
wearing thorns for their protection,
leave long red streaks on thieving hands.
But in a cobbler, oven hot,
the treasured stolen purple fruit
yields juicy flavored sweetness.
Stricken by November frost,
my shriveled grapes hang frozen
on twisted, leafless vines.
But picked with love
and aged with vintner's skill,
their ice-wine charms our palates.
So too when skies stay gray
and politics bring deep despair
and loneliness prevails,
remember that the sun will shine,
statesmen true will soon arise,
and friends bring joy and solace.

Red Fox in the Orchard

Red fox in the orchard
Proud, tail flowing in the wind,
Ate up the Gingerbread Boy,
Tricked the bear to freeze
Its tail in the ice.
Stately, subverts
The status quo.
A moment of beauty
To the surprised eyes
Behind the window pane.

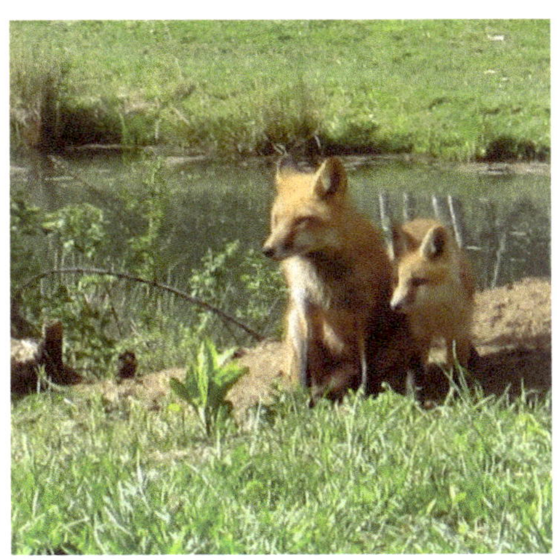

Sunrise on the Beach

Orange glow inches high above marsh grass.
Thin crescent moon in east begins to fade.
October north wind whips up whitecaps.
A great egret floats from cedar branch to water's edge,
as pods of dolphin synchronize gray dorsal sails,
then disappear again beneath the waves.
Backs to the wind,
blue-checked towels for seats,
we watch as cordgrass turns in rising sun
from brown to glowing gold,
and flocks of seagulls swoop and laugh.
We hear the leaping croakers splash
and wavelets lap against the sand.
Dawn comes later now each autumn morn,
not one alike, colors linked to clouds and mist,
but faithful to earth's cosmic laws
as inlet fills or tide recedes:
there's certainty of permanence
and constant joy of welcome change.
So, bundled up against chill winds,
eyes bright in sunrise glow,
we greet the dawning seaside hours
with gratitude for sights and sounds,
with anticipation of a day well spent,
and wondrous harmony of life and love.

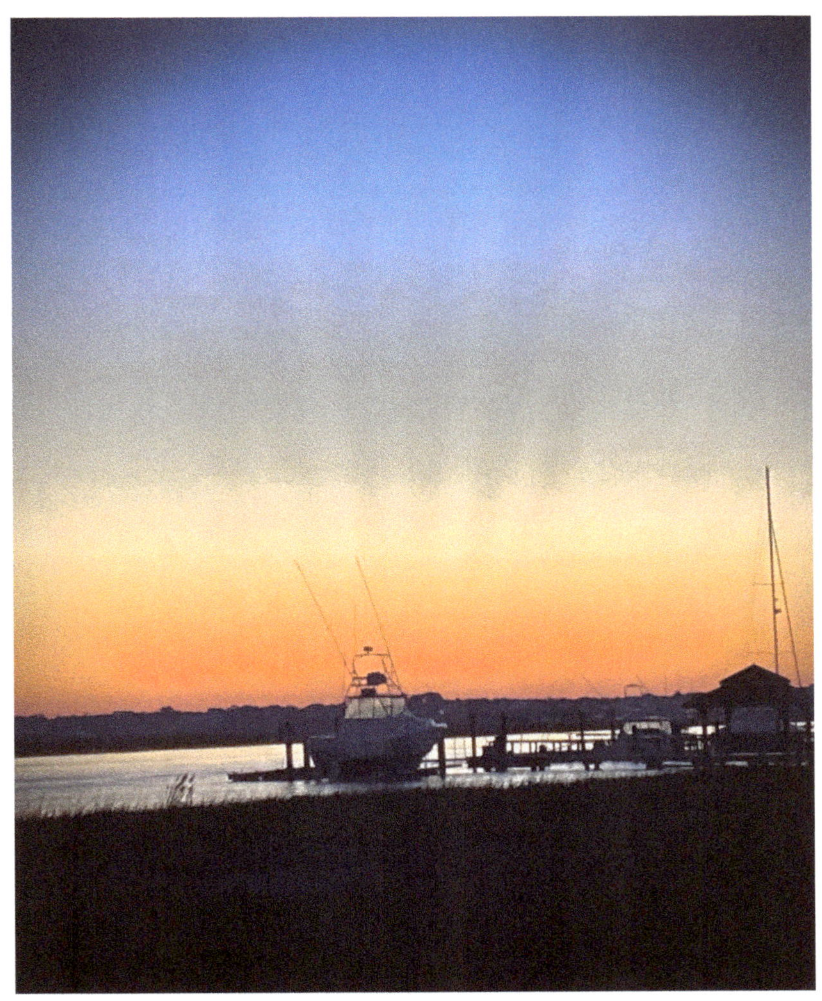

Screech Owls

Sturdy mountain silhouetted against last glow in west,
Jupiter hangs bright in cold eastern sky,
staring down on quiet November evening
as we make our nightly round,
kept warm by soft wool scarves.

We catch a movement
and watch in wonder as
on silent wings a screech owl glides
through cold shadows, coming to rest
midst leaves still clinging tight to scarlet oak.

No cheery, soothing song to human ears,
more like screech of metal,
but music to his mate in nearby tree,
who gives throat to welcome answers
with her low pitch antiphonal trill.

Now perched close like turtle doves,
they clutch their branch
and together watch reflected in wide eyes
the half-moon poised above
and us breathless below.

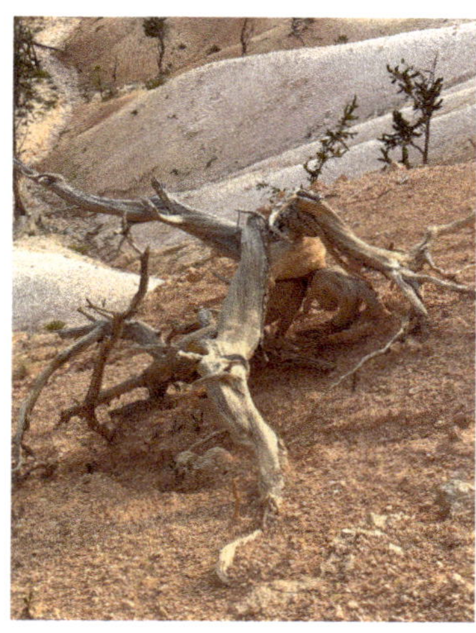

Ode to Moss

Infinite varieties on multifacet bases,
Here, pale green threads, you cling to sheer rock faces;
There, you offer soft green cushion under our bare feet,
Spreading over hillside on every fold and pleat.
Like pilgrim humans 'neath a wandering star,
You set no roots, when drifting from afar,
Yet true adapter, you always find your homes
And cling to any surface just with small rhizomes.
Were I, like Gulliver in Lilliputian land,
To creep ant-like through mammoth stem and strand,
I'd be like man in massive forest tall,
Where oaks and chestnuts hold us in their thrall.
In times of drought, like our pandemic past,
You hunker down, to live, to last,
Awaiting rain, like friends' outpouring love,
New life sustained with manna from above.
Oh, humble moss, no towering beacon light,
No cymbals clashing, no soaring lofty flight,
You model hope, toward which each human strives,
For love, like rain, enriches all our lives.

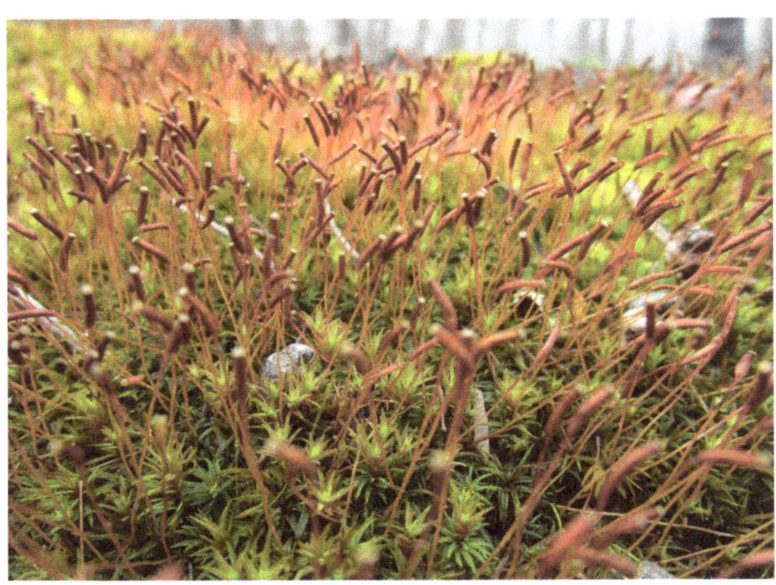

A Winter Blessing for My Friends

When the clouds hang low over our dark mountains
And memories of losses invade our hearts,
When the weight of determining truth is unbearable
And we witness waste and destruction of our earthly home,
When our visits to health care become more frequent
And our thoughts rest on what might have been,
May you awake tomorrow to the songs of the wren,
Reminding you of the beauty of small things,
That melodies await our open ears.
And may you witness the majestic flight
Of the blue heron as it rises from our pond,
Neck curved and legs extended,
Lifting earthbound body into lightness.
And one day, after the clouds have gone,
May you marvel at the snow-capped peaks
Rising toward celestial azure like cathedral spires.
And most of all,
May you know that though grief is lasting,
Loneliness is but fleeting, and so
May you bask in the warmth of friendship,
Alert to the winking smile and the tender touch
Of your companions on this journey.
May you feel secure in the arms of community,
Sharing days both difficult and joyous.
May you know that nothing can separate you
 From the love of comrades nor of the Divine.

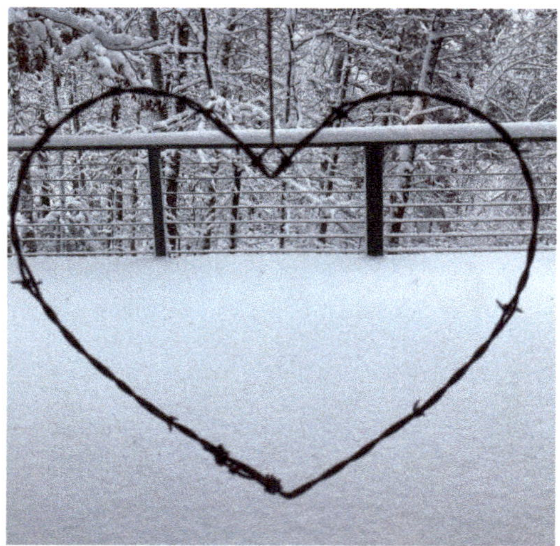

Daughter in Winter
(inspired by Catalan poet Joan Margarit)

Snow pelting in that raging blizzard,
We started carefully down the long road south
Along the heartland river,
Glancing back and forth at each other
In January wonderment.

Within us we can still recall
the blizzard change to flurries,
then to cloudless azure sky,
and finally grime-streaked car
rolling under waving green palm fronds.

We still can see
the midwife lifting up
in swaddling clothes
an infant with black forehead curl,
dark eyes open wide,
daughter only four days old
and already a winning smile.

Today I watch that infant girl
facing life with strength mature,
weathering winter storms herself,
her dark eyes radiating courage,
reminder of the timid love
born that day in southern climes
and grown to everlasting fullness.

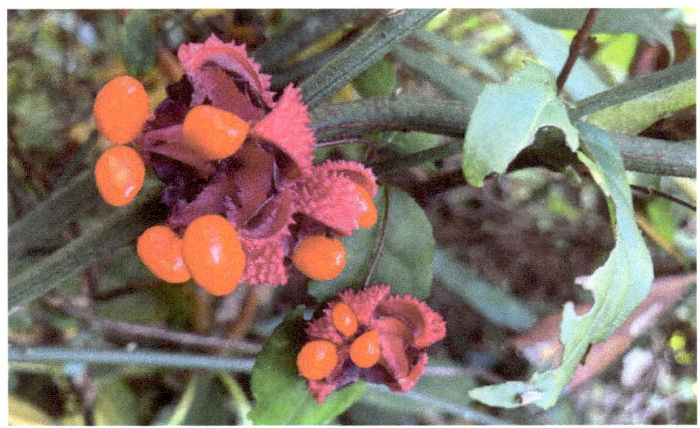

Son in Spring
(Inspired by Catalan poet Joan Margarit)

Neath the spreading branches of the mango tree,
heavily laden with gold and purple fruits,
full setting moon filtering through glistening leaves,
you lie, cradled in mother's arms,
slowly moving on a simple truck bed,
as night begins to gray,
toward nearby welcoming guest house
from hospital on your first short trek
along dark flowing Kwilu River,
watched by resident crocs and hippos,
you now fast asleep and quiet after first shocked cry
awakening to the equatorial world.

Next day, a longer dusty road,
sleeping in wicker basket
on back seat of rusty Volkswagen
on red laterite roads
past tall termite mounds
under towering jungle trees
where squawking hornbills vied for food
and lilac-breasted rollers flashed their blue and purple wings;
then a ferry on well-worn cable,
pulled by flowing current from bank to bank
to reach new home
and bed by candlelight,
lulled by neighborhood drumbeats.

Then, tiny infant,
newly minted life,
now, strong, adventuresome,
embarked on other journeys,
seeking out the marvels our grand world displays:
a snowy torch-lit alpine Christmas trek,
the peaks of 14,000 feet
in Colorado, sometimes in snow,
camino pilgrimage at Eastertide,
and now exploring ancient Moorish Spain,
enjoying paella, gold with saffron,
and flamenco dancers, scarlet clothed;
then drifting off in slumber,
dreaming of new adventures,
to the rhythm of castanets.

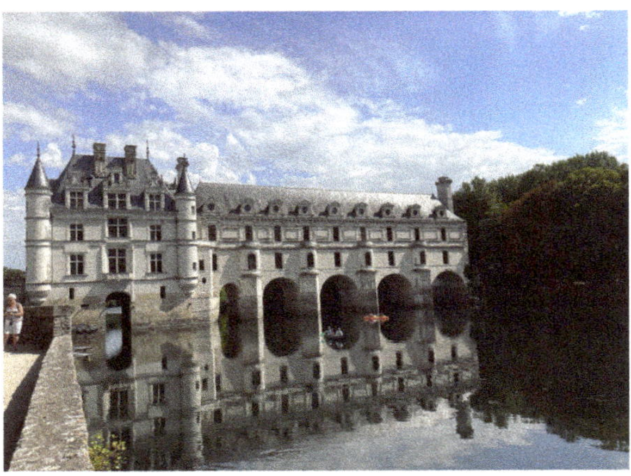

A Morning Blessing

On days the morning fog veils our mountains
May you consider the mysteries it hides
And may you rest in its protection

Or when the golden morning sun
traces first wispy sheen to outline clouds
May your eyes embrace nature's palette

When the hummingbirds perform
their early acrobatic loops
May you be grateful for lithe limbs

When the shadow of the ancient oak
stretches toward the setting moon
May you remember those who've come before you

When sister wren begins her cheery song
May your heart be lifted up and
May you too raise a hymn of joy

As the dawning day offers fresh new options
May you forget the weighty cares of yesterday
And may your mind fling wide its gates

When our verdant valley stirs awake
to train's distant echoing whistles
May you be attuned to hear soft words of love

Tastefully

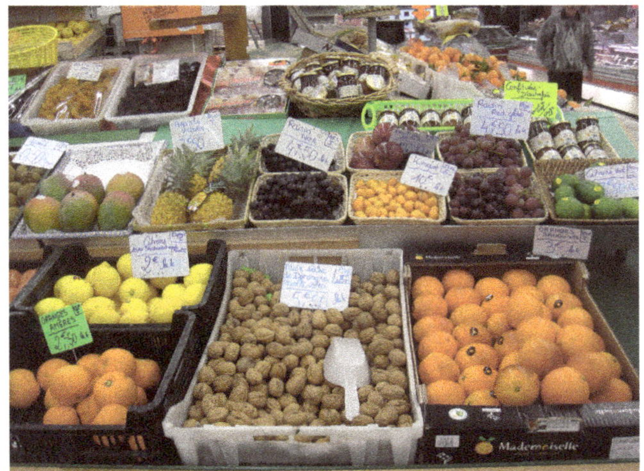

In this Thanksgiving season
I offer thanks for savors,
for tastes that waken memories,
like Marcel Proust's remembered world
in teacup's sip renewed.

For peppery oyster stew my father made in winter,
for omelettes laced with aromatic truffles
bought in the streets of Mont St. Michel;
for juicy Christmas grapefruits, ruby red,
our grandpa sent from warmer climes;
for buckwheat crepes, Nutella filled,
savored hot by Paris sidewalk stands
with steaming demi-tasse of rich espresso.

And now, today, remember grateful ritual
of crimson sauce, its berries sweetly sour,
of peppery stuffing enhanced with sage
and steaming meaty gravies
over crisp-skinned turkey breast.
This cheery tasteful table
brings smiles and nods of joy,
awakens tuneful melodies,
evoking sweet deep harmony,
uniting friends and kin.

2020 Vision

My vision is no longer 20/20,
but I'm pleased to see clearly
in this year 2020
that in spite of viral plague,
misinformation, armed conflict,
and financial insecurity,
my eyes still notice beauty, smiles,
and acts of kindness and solidarity.

Though life has seemed more tenuous,
I, unlike many, faced not
the stress of job loss and
disappearing health insurance.
And I was spared even the loneliness
of self-isolation and confinement
as new partner graced my life,
each building on loves once lived.

Together we created joy and wonder,
exploring mountain trails,
seeking form and color
through camera lens
and the lens of happiness.
An April creekside ceremony
with no family but a few masked friends
confirmed commitment.

Grateful too I was in summer
for skilled surgeon's touch,
repairing wrist and tendons
and for therapy restoring strength
and motion,
allowing ukulele strum
and veggie chopping.

Pandemic cancelled
two-week walking trip in France
along river bank 'neath castle turrets.
Those walks replaced
by sunrise strolls à deux
on sandy Carolina strands.
No crêpes nor chèvre
but thanks I raise
for tasty shrimp and key lime pie.

This year no family Thanksgiving turkey
Nor extended indoor table
laden with potatoes, golden corn,
cranberries red, and pumpkin pie.
A new adventure en plein air,
complete with racks of ribs,
with sides and sauce
from aptly named Twelve Bones.

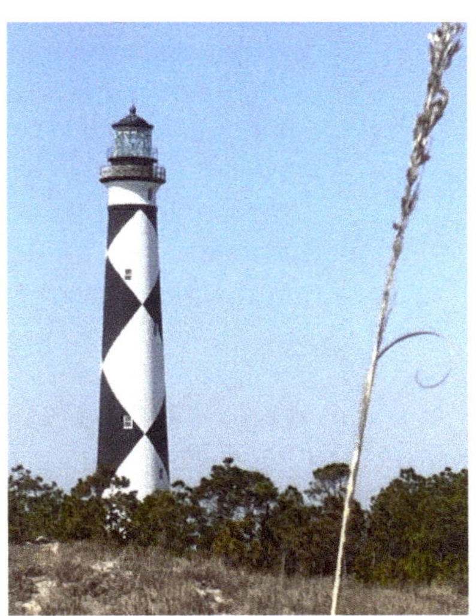

Deep joy and gratitude profound
abound for cozy dwelling place
that overlooks a pond
visited by my totem heron,
a belted kingfisher,
and geese in gaggles.
I offer thanks for a sunny study
with windows opening
on to graceful mountain ridges
and autumn's colors
replicated on warm indoor walls,
graced by artist's shapes and hues.

Gratitude
(with gratitude and apologies to Mary Oliver!)

What have you heard?

The mockingbird at midnight,
a beaver's slapping tail in Gem Creek,
the cicada's rasping on parasol pine,
the lonely train whistle just before dawn,
from the minaret, a muezzin's call to prayer,
our bluebird tapping at the window,
pounding wildebeest hooves during migration,
bugling elk on Colorado slopes or Cataloochee Valley,
the hen celebrating her oval gift,
a circling Cooper's hawk invoking "kir,"
church bells in an Alpine village on Christmas Eve,
Leonard Cohen's "Hallelujah,"
a throaty lion roar at Serengeti dawn,
the lonely loon on Red Shirt Lake,
the soothing voice of the beloved,
and the profound quiet of falling snow.

What would you like to see again?

The first bloodroot in spring,
hoarfrost on Jura spruces,
the snows of Kilimanjaro,
the purple underside of cranefly orchid leaves,
white salt mounds along the Brittany coast,
twelve winter bluebirds erupting from the backyard house,
the spires of Santiago from nearby hill,
the dark snouts of waiting crocodiles in Lake Tanganyika,
the structure of moss cells through microscope,
the puff of spores from brown puffballs,
Moroccan goats peering down from trees,
lilacs growing on thatched roof homes,
the red-tailed hawk with writhing snake in talons,
Christ in Majesty in romanesque tympana,
red roses at each end of green vineyard rows,
the twisted sculpture of sourwood seeking sunlight,
full harvest moon rising over Dinali,
the beloved dipping canoe paddle
to join our resident swans.

What tastes or scents?

Sweet honey fresh from the honeycomb,
licked from the beloved's finger,
Proust's memory-laden madeleines,
the cleansing ozone after summer storm,
the sharp perfume of trodden Galax leaves,
the bowl of cider's biting crispness,
pearl onions in my coq au vin,
the heady iodine from ocean waves,
the sweetness of roasted Brussels sprouts,
or salty mold in Roquefort cheese,
the rising smoke from white oak logs
on cloudless winter days.

May I always live in gratitude
and not forget the joys
of image, sound, and scent,
of time with the beloved,
gracious, sacred gifts of the Creator
to make my life complete.

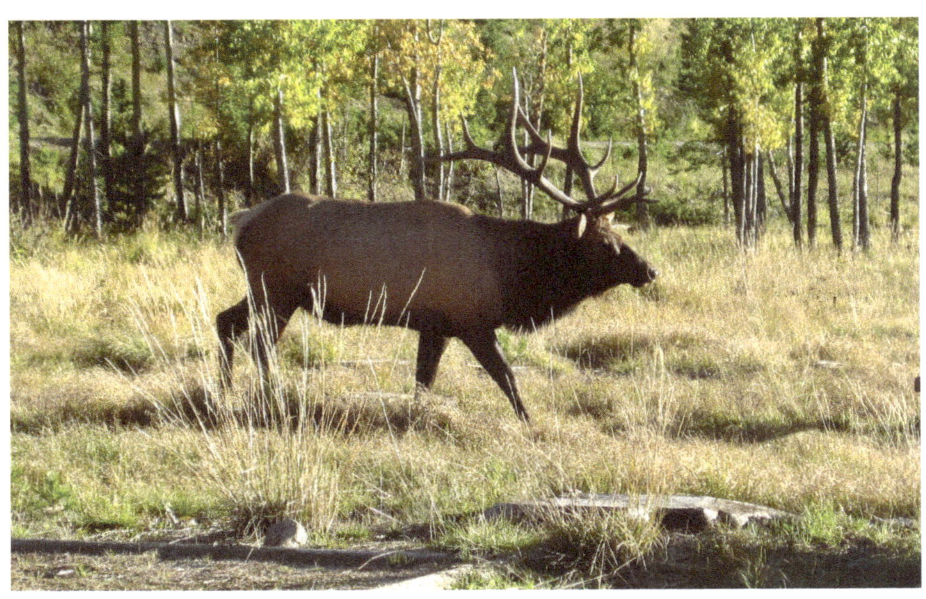

October in Sleeping Bear Dunes

The autumn wind lifts whitecaps from blue lake,
then sets red maple leaves aquiver;
fine sand stings face when lifted over sandy tops,
moving massive Sleeping Bear dunes slowly eastward.

A bald eagle, tail feathers flashing white in sun,
harassed by pesky diving tern,
nonchalantly soars against azure sky.
Like a migratory swan, you venture north
Once more from warmer Carolina climes,
remembering life midst rows of cherry trees,
children splashing in crystalline lakes,
artists' galleries, and warmth of friends.

Now strong legs tread white beaches
strewn with rounded rocks blue, white, or gray,
or deep forest paths thick with mushrooms,
stopping with camera in hand for pattern and color,
ear attuned to drumming woodpeckers,
the belted kingfisher's staccato call,
the whistling wind in treetops,
and the pounding waves on lakeshore sand.

Roadsides sport pumpkins, white and golden,
Primed for carving toothy grins,
along with sheaves of Indian corn, hues red and blue.
Crimson sunset colors patchy clouds before
as full-sprung rainbow surprises from behind.

At night Ursa Major dominates the northern sky,
Her dipper upright to catch autumn rains.
Above our heads stretches glorious Milky Way,
its myriad galaxies spread through time and space.

Tree-covered dunes doze like massive bears
along a lake carved out by glacier's path,
awakening memories of children's gleeful shouts
as cold clear water beckoned,
or flashbacks to fabrics, warp and woof,
and cheerful studio days shared with sister minds.

All this—nature, color, art, and love
you share, incorporating richly textured past
with present, live and flourishing.

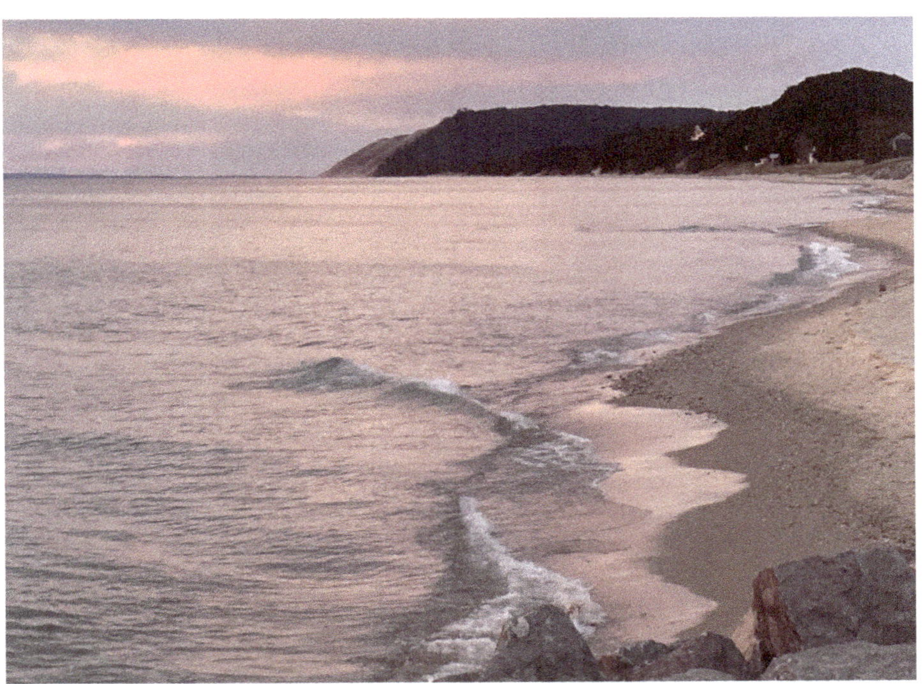

Blueberry Winter

It's now mid-winter,
and your crimson foliage
has long before
floated down to the oak mulch,
protecting your shallow roots.

When days are short,
pruner in hand,
I shear unnecessary growth,
removing dry twigs
and crossing branches,
wondering how such lifeless wood
will ever yield its bounty.

The nights are long now,
and when the wind is calm,
our barred owl
glides silently through the trees,
ever alert for movement
beneath the bushes bare.

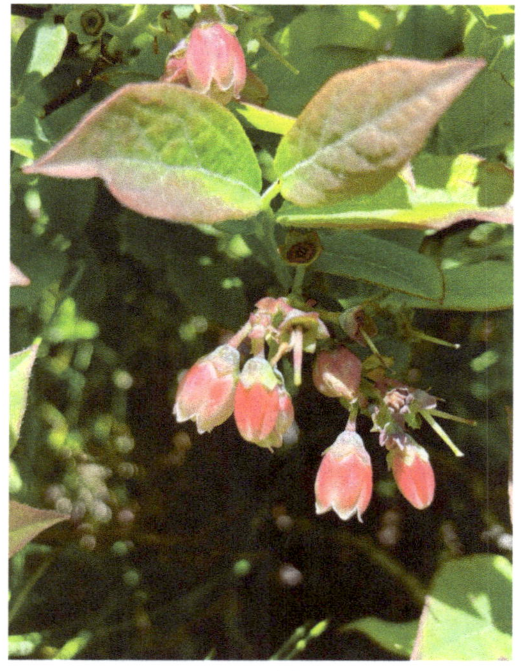

But I remember
from years past,
that even in February,
the tips of twigs
begin to swell,
harbingers of spring,
of white blossoms,
themselves precursors
of fruit pink,
like a rabbit's eye.

If barren branches
hold such promise,
the gray winter of my discontent
will waken,
as the ground grows warm,
to springtime's tints
and the cheery trill
of sister wren.

And as the summer rains
roll in,
and days grow long,
pink turns blue
and sweet swollen berries
hang profusely from strong branches,
calling to flocks of robins,
attracting inquisitive fawns,
and yielding
to stained fingers
filling pails and mouths.

Valentine's Day 2022

Some express their love with chocolates
inscribed with "Be My Valentine."
Some may speak with posies,
red roses, or carnations.

Though I may speak at times with both,
please sense my love, agape too with eros,
with walks on evening's darkened streets,
not distant, with space between
as Dog Star follows belted hunter
in February's clear night sky,
but arm in arm, together,
your soul in touch with mine.

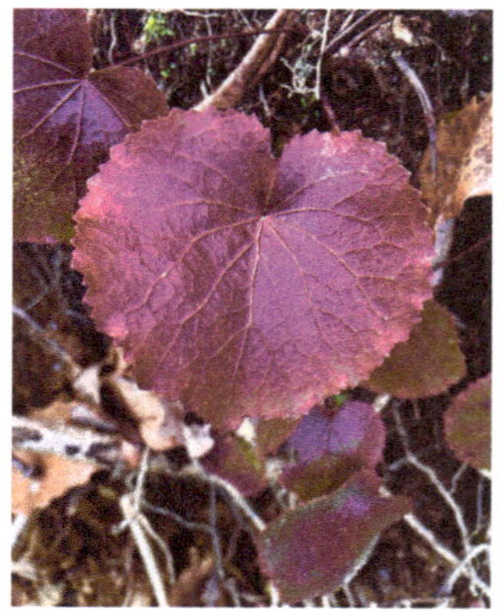

And sense it too
on frigid morning hikes,
scarf warmed and glove in glove,
when sparkling eyes
watch contrails crisscross morning's glory,
and pink clouds crown our mountains,
we move with steps in synchrony,
ears pealed for early bluebird songs
announcing avian joy.

My love's expressed
in word-game competitions too.
On-line fields of verbal play
bring challenge and delight
when I best you or you best me,
the loser's prize a kiss.

So this day, my love, brings gifts—
a rose, a truffled chocolate,
a walk at dawn and dusk.
When one wins with words,
The other wins the prize!

Maracuja (Passion Fruit)

Some years,
As Easter time awakes
The dogwood blooms
in Carolina
And speaks of blood
On petals white
Its hard dense wood
Ideal to bear the weight.

This year
On Easter morn
in Kenyan hills
The cross shows mauve
On delicate white
A passion flower
Its viney fingers
Reach with hope
Will bear sweet fruit.

Maracuja
Mara tutakapokuja
"When will we come"
And share
The red
The mauve
The pain
The hope?

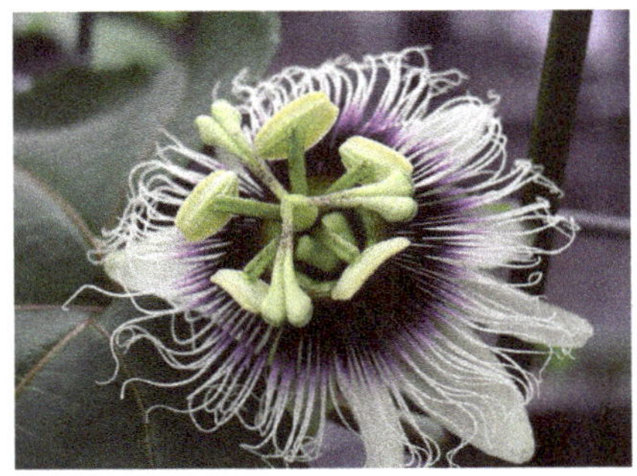

Spring Colors on the Farm

It's early March,
and on this morning's walk
I spot the first new trillium,
wild toadshades,
with maroon bloom announced
but yet unsheathed.

Against the thick gray mountain fog
deep red blossoms
blanket the spreading crowns
of campus maple trees,
foretelling myriad helicopter seeds
to nourish summer's cedar waxwings,
wings golden in the sun,
and future growth
of stately trunks.

In human-tended gardens,
blue crocus
and grape hyacinths
push up near golden daffodils,
reflecting tender love
and bringing beauty
to every eye.

On the tall grass
around pond's rim
blackbird perches,
newly arrived from warmer lands,
showing off from time to time,
bright orange-red bars
on black wings.

Male bluebird rests on nearby branch
or works at suet cage,
reddish breast and white belly
neath rich iridescent blue,
his liquid warble,
an ode to madam,
a soft and simple morning song.

And on Nature's Trail,
clustered on mottled green-gray leaves,
spring's first yellow trout lilies
now vie for our attention
with nearby gold-stamened
white Oconee Bells,
on deep-green leaves like Galax,
red-tipped,
looking for all the world
like small shuttlecocks.

Designed
for ant and bee attraction
or combined with song for seeking mates,
these colors,
uncowed by greed and plague,
delight the human soul as well,
bringing peace, joy,
and recognition
that Nature's cycle springs,
like hope, eternal.

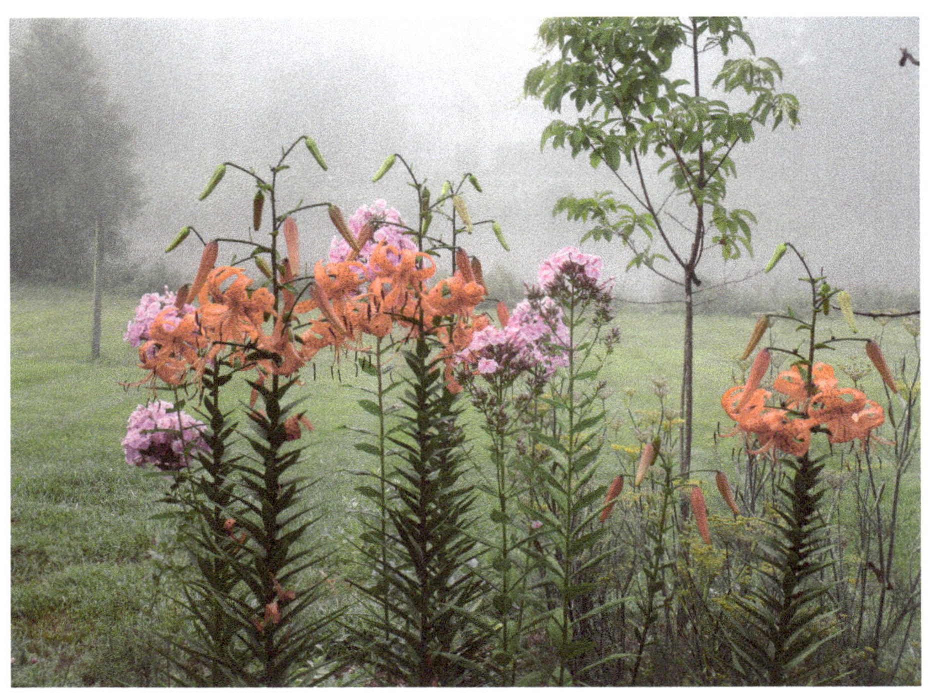

December Sky

The glow in the west fades earlier now,
may turn us inward toward much darker places.
But even after sun disappears 'neath horizon,
the belt of Venus keeps hope alive
in shades of mauve and pink
above mountain tops in eastern sky.

And then in these dark winter heavens,
we watch three planets
inching nightly on their western path,
bathing us in diffuse reflected light
and lightly molding our deepest wishes.

Jupiter stands tall overhead,
jovial, noble, dignified,
bringer of good fortune
presiding over the earth,
encouraging respect for self and others.

He looks down towards his father,
Saturn, lower in the west,
dimmer, darker,
though not always saturnine,
but a symbol of patience,
hard work, and perseverance,
god of history and maturity,
thus welcome to our fourscore years.

And beautiful Venus,
now the evening star,
brightest creature in the heavens,
save her lunar cohort,
proclaiming love and honoring beauty,
reminding us of life's beckoning pleasures.

And tonight the waxing crescent moon
shines down from next to noble Jupiter.
She speaks of cycles
of blessed lunatic behavior,
spontaneity, and whimsical adventures,
providing moon-struck joy,
that make us truly human.

And now as well, in mid-December,
as half-moon completes
its late night westerly descent,
meteoric flashes fill the sky,
Geminid gifts in shower,
a travelling comet's witness
to our infinite universe,
a reminder both of August Perseids
in clear Coloradan skies
and of you and me as infinitismal beings
on home planet Earth.

Tiny, yes, and hardly specks of dust
but also joyfully alive,
reaching far beyond ourselves,
sensing connection with specks of light,
with ancient myth and mages,
and with our wondrous universe
spread out in winter's sky.

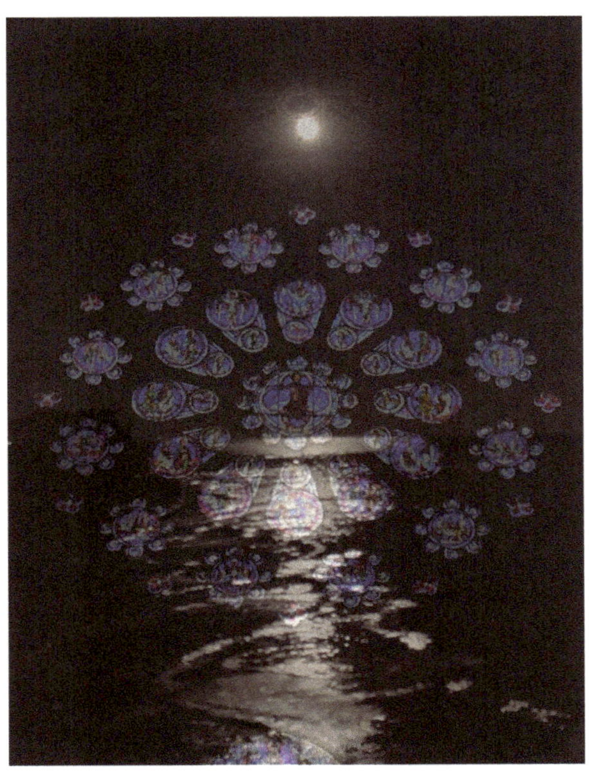

The Thorn Candle

In my Virginia mind
A crown of thorns?
No doubt of blackberry,
Limber berry canes.
Thorns, yes, but small
Not perfumed
Like honeysuckle wreaths
And only prickly to wear
Embarrassing perhaps
Not agony.

This day in Africa
On a Nairobi table
Not fronds of palm
In triumph
Nor victor's laurel wreaths
But a crown of thorn acacia
With three-inch nails
Deadly
Not to giraffes
With tender tongues
But pain to Man
With tender brow
Each thorn real
A sharp reminder
Of human suffering
Thatched roofs in flame
Hostage to ideology
The unknown occupants
Of mass graves.

From acacia-punctured brow
Drips real blood
The book of Africa.
Yet through genocide
And hecatomb
Rising amid long thorns
At Easter time
On a friend's table
In a crown of thorns
A glowing candle
Proclaims
Our hope.

Snow in March

Once more frosting on the wood pile
The rocky stream bubbling through falling flakes
White-capped rocks holding heads above ripples
The crimson cardinal watches from the forsythia
budding yellow on the hill
Wrens and downy woodpecker complete relays to the suet
Drab winter lawn is white-washed away
Mud and brown crabgrass enhanced cosmetically
Quiet on the road, cars waiting in their garages
For the snow on the mountain to disappear.
Warm before the fire,
We sit hand in hand
And watch the miracle unfold again
Outside our window.

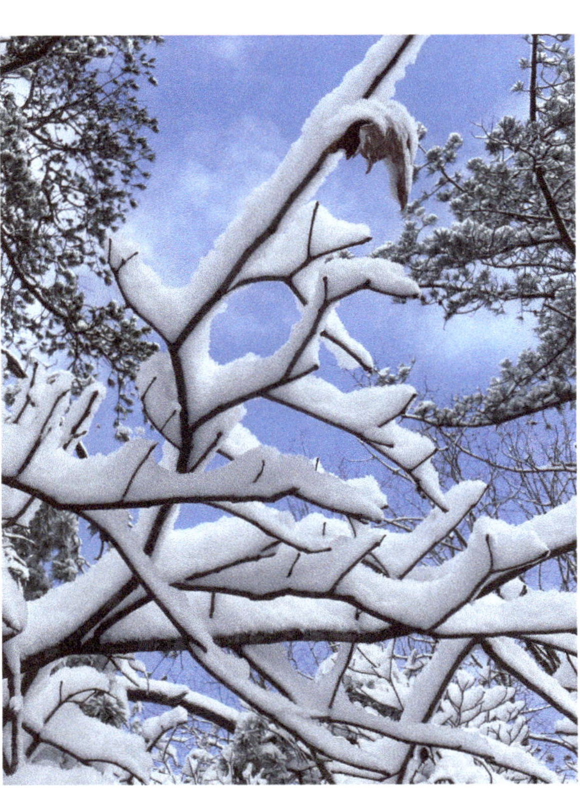

Pilgrims

In 1019 you left Le Puy or Vézelay,
staff in right hand, water gourd at belt,
wide-brimmed hat to block both sun and rain.
A thousand miles ahead,
following an unmarked trail,
your goal of Santiago to prove your faith.

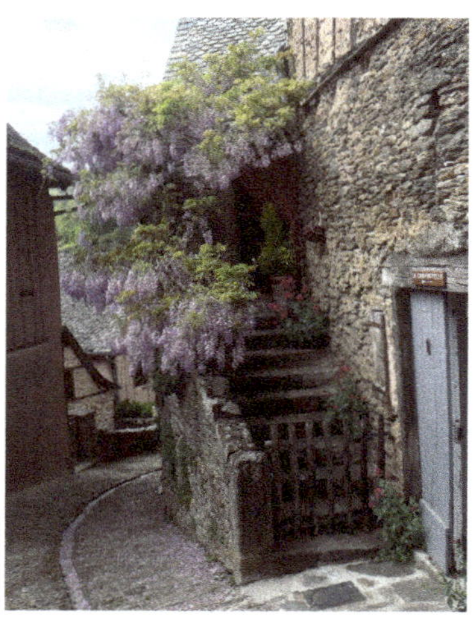

When possible, you walked in groups,
fearing highwaymen and cutthroats.
In your bag, some hard cheese and bread,
enough, you thought,
for those you met would do their duty
and help all pilgrims.

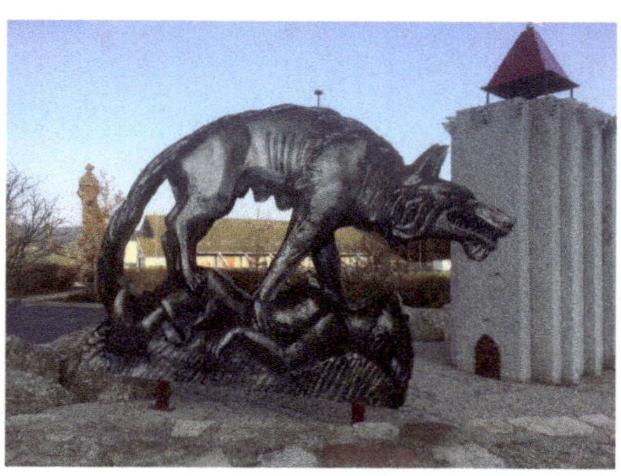

At night you lay 'neath trees,
in rocky fields,
wrapping cloak around you.
Some fortunate nights
a village candle
lit the path to a small church
and shelter from the chill of night.
Or even better, the wind
wafted from a monastery kitchen
the promise of warm soup.

Each day you thanked your God
for miles behind you,
for safety on the path,
for sustenance, both
material and spiritual.

A thousand years later in Le Puy-en-Velay
I left the gray stone cathedral
and its black madonna
one day in April,
slowly descending the staircase
to begin my own pilgrimage
on the first legs of the trail to Santiago.
Perhaps to prove my faith,
perhaps to honor my life partner
who respected religious seeking
and longed to live in harmony
with nature.

I walked through field and forest,
over ancient dark volcanic rock,
on trail well marked with red and white.
An immense plateau where
in the 18th Century
a fearsome creature ravaged
man and beast
in the Gévaudan.
Deep river gorges
and broad mountain meadows
where cows, now content in valley barns,
will graze in summer,
and where the cowherds
will make tasty mountain cheeses.

Sometimes the pastures
were festooned with wild daffodils,
standing small but strong
among the grey boulders.
At times I passed
groves of ancient chestnut trees,
planted 150 years ago
and providers of food for generations.

Late each afternoon,
as legs tired and back ached,
over the crest of a hill
I was cheered to see
grey granite buildings clustered
around a church steeple,
the day's destination.
And if the town was large enough,
the trail led past bakery
or cheese shop,
whetting the appetite for an evening meal.

You, the early pilgrim
slept where darkness found you,
surely sometimes with pangs of hunger.
I, completing my allotted
ten to sixteen miles,
always found a tasty meal waiting,
a soft hotel bed,
and croissants for breakfast.

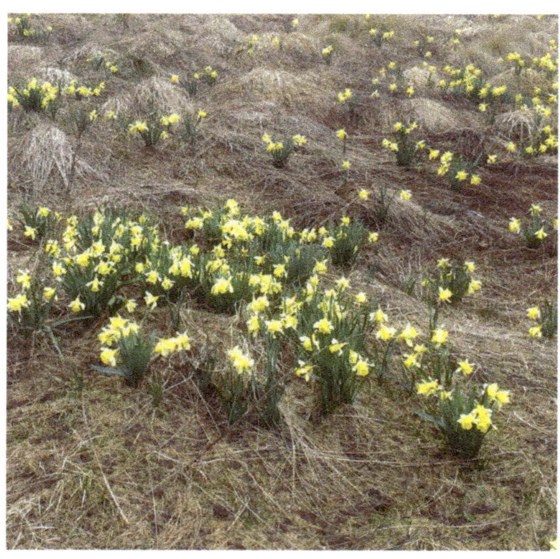

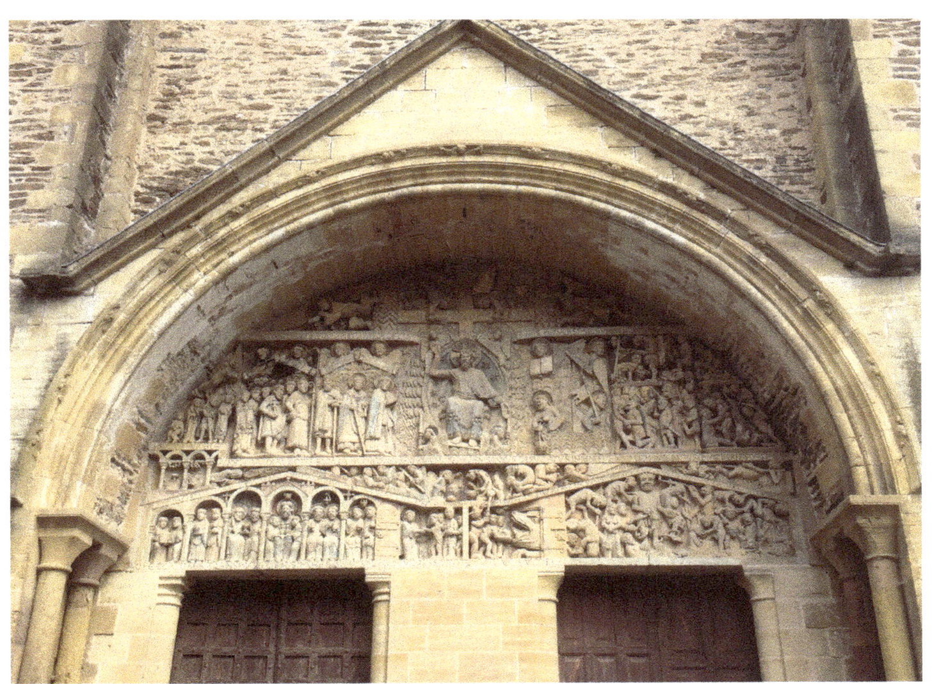

You, sometimes walked
in sodden cloak,
and open sandals.
But I, in modern hiking boots
and hooded rain jacket,
kept mostly dry
even during my four days
of rain, of sleet, of snow.

I did not reach Santiago,
could not claim be the king
because the first to see cathedral spires.
But I did,
on a sunny, windy afternoon,
walk down into Conques,
a pilgrimage site itself for us,
our favorite French village
with narrow medieval streets,
its romanesque Sainte Foy church
and its tympanum with Christ in Majesty.
And I could claim my faith in love
and honor the memory of my beloved.

Testament (RSY)

I leave you a world,
A world we both have learned to love:
Magic and sleight of hand
Brews both dark and white
A hike in snow
Chocolate eclairs and Dijon mustard
A smile and words in French
Shared joys of volleyball
in gyms or on a Kenyan beach
Memories of Briarpatch
of sleds and skis
of yellow jacket nests
Afternoons chopping onions
for onion tart or coq au vin
Scratching in the waiting earth
to scatter seeds for future salads
Jumping into the warm water
of a Gabonese bay
after a dusty road trip
Exploring Colorado mountains
and discovering hidden lakes
and columbines, both blue and yellow,
Music from requiems to Renaud,
from Sting to Schubert.

And I leave you a world
that also brought
its pain and hardships,
inching us toward humility,
compassion, and understanding.
A world where homeless seek survival
on Haitian and Atlantan streets,
A world where loved ones
lose their fight with death.
Remember both the happy days
and shared sad tears.

To you our son,
I bequeath
a ready smile,
a quest for justice,
a zest for living,
an acceptance of self,
and a heart full of peace.

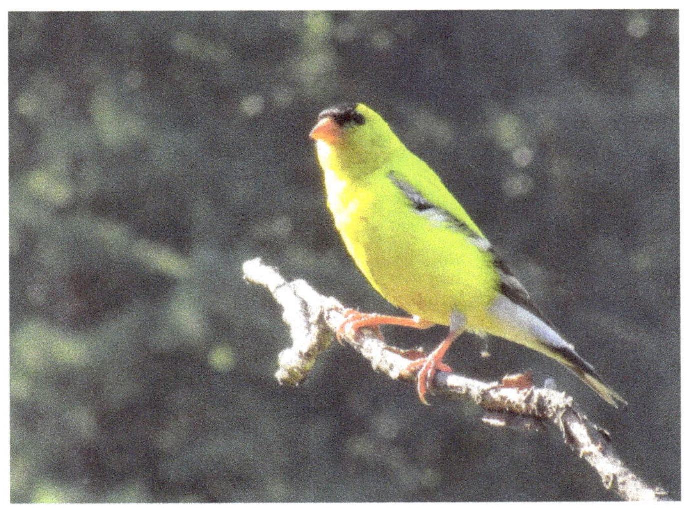

Testament (JVY)

I leave you a world
We both have learned to love.

Tasty blueberries
from laden bushes
Memories of making "stews"
on garden paths
behind brown house.
You with watering-can
by mammoth oak
so it would live
and not fall on your room,
preparation for future days
as plant specialist
in garden center.

We remember walking together,
snow falling
in Alpine village
or early morning
hand in hand on streets
toward kindergarten in Montpellier
or school in Davidson.

Special picnics,
with sandwiches
on Carolina mountain trails,
Quiche and éclairs au chocolat
from French pastry shops
enjoyed under ancient chestnuts
in the Cévennes hills,
Red finger-size bananas
and mangoes dripping juice
on the Ogooué River
downstream from Lambarene,
Schweitzer's hospital,
and David's baby gorilla.
Shared comfort food—
toasted cheese with poppy seeds
and tomato soup

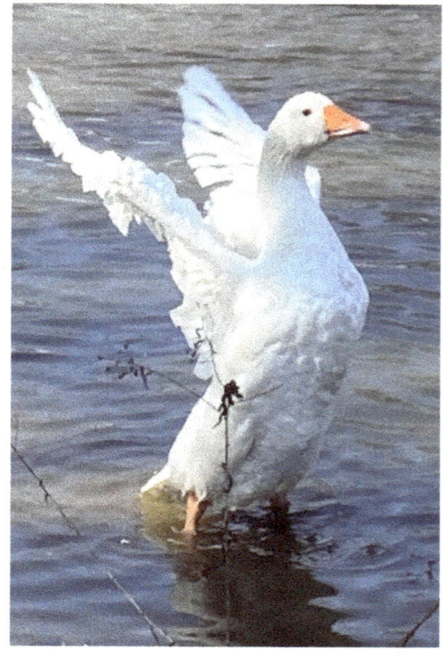

with fresh rosemary sprigs,
or scalloped potatoes
made by mother's loving hand,
and perhaps my coq au vin.

We both have pictures in our mind
of weeks in Haiti,
rushing out with bars of soap
to bathe in downpours,
eating fresh, green watercress
and rice red with tomato paste,
and you
captured by camera,
seated between two baby goats.

The world we loved
also brought pain,
and with the pain
humility and recognition
that we need each other.
Remember those first mornings
waiting for the bus together for junior high
when dread
filled your heart,
the shock to you and us
of the oncologist's call
announcing bad news,
and those painful weeks
we shared with mom and spouse
as illness sapped her strength
but not her soul.

Remembering joys and sorrows,
from the first morning in Mississippi
through days in France and Africa
and life in Carolina,
to you our true daughter
I bequeath
an eye for beauty,
a mind for curiosity,
a hand for helping,
and a heart for peace.

Akamba Bus

A path toward peace?
Like a highway
With broken pavement
Side eaten away
No center line of course
Potholes, nids de poule.

A chicken in every pot?
Lucky to have matoke or posho
Not chicken
But at the the window
Of the bus
Fast food?
A hand stretches up
Beyond a smiling hopeful face
Clutching, like flags
Chicken-on-a-stick
Roast chicken breast
With pilipili
I sell my chicken
My children
Eat today!

On the narrow road
Antagonists play chicken
At breakneck speed.
Which will yield?
My Nissan van
Or the big yellow/green Akamba bus?
The weaker
Pulls to the shoulder
Lamenting time lost.
The yellow-green monster rolls on
Like the rebel army
Mucking through the rains
Towards Kisangani
Nature abhors a vacuum.

Which way peace?
No center line
To follow
Our direction wavers
Around a curve
The lines mound up and cross
Confusion
Black and white not clear at all
Dead zebra on the road
Not every line says "follow"
We pick our way.
Which path toward peace?

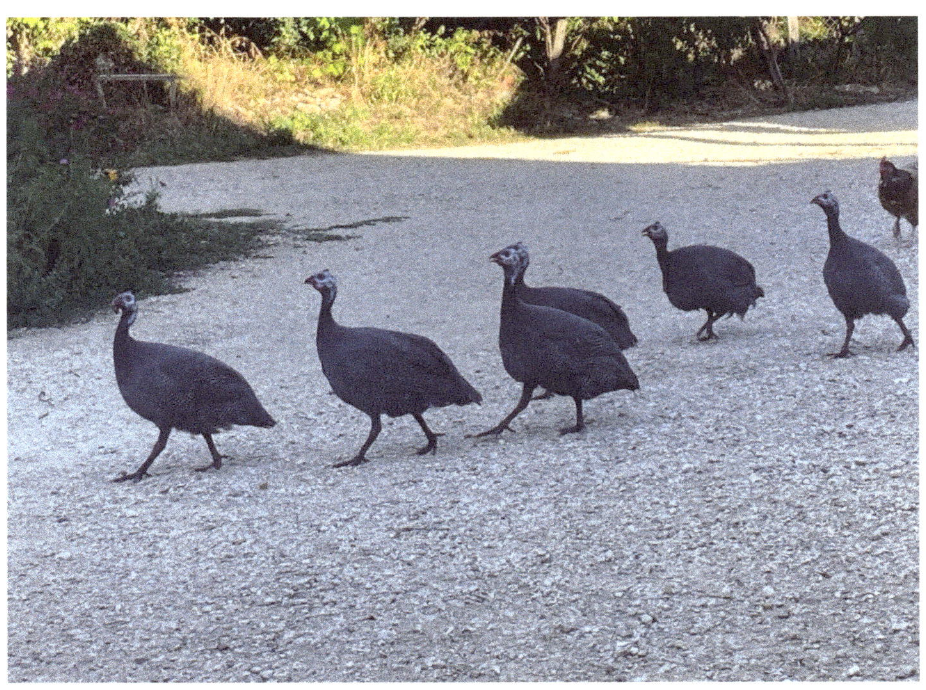

Enemy Brothers

I watched
This morning
Two lizards, small dragons,
Grey and red
Between two rains,
Enjoying warmth of sun.

Two ordinary lizards
Alike in every way.
Red heads,
Grey bodies.
Both love sunshine,
Both love ants.

Slowly they turned
And faced each other.
What thoughts
Coursed through
Their minds?

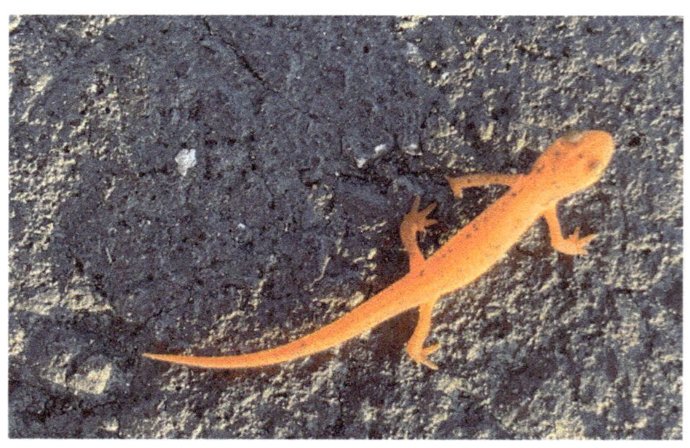

A stolen ant?
Not sun enough for both?

A baleful eye
Triggers hate,
And violence
Explodes.
Toothless mouth rips
Toothless mouth.
Claws rake on flesh.
Spasms of rage,
They silently roar.
One pinned on his back
Four feet slashing
And flips his brother.
No victor yet.
Then strong jaws clamp
On soft underbelly.

Tearing free,
One red grey lizard
Rushes off behind
A pile of rocks.
His red grey brother
Stands proudly
Head raised
Doing lizard push-ups.
Abel, Cain,
Tutsi, Hutu,
Enemy brothers.
The battle over,
He'll live in pride.

Some minutes later
From behind the rocks
A grey red lizard
Creeps slowly out.
His wounds licked,
He watches, stares,
And waits his chance.
Must surely try again
To be top dog lizard.

Long Rain

The old Maasai herder
Along the dusty path
Sits waiting,
Knobbed stick in calloused hand.
"We live in cycles,"
He says drily,
"Now no water,
But rains will come."
If knobbed stick
Strikes the rock,
Will springs gush forth?

The long rains
Long in coming
Yellow stunted cornstalks
At nearly dry
Water holes.
Herds of cattle
Weak and thin
Fight for
Muddy draughts
With goats
And donkeys.
Vultures
And marabout storks
Watch
From leafless trees.
Black earth
Fissured
Pulverized
Blowing in gusts
Under cloudless skies.
Floods in Zambia.
Mozambique soggy,
There rains tarry,
Where prayers were
Too effective.
Did magic work?

This week in Kenya
A diviner
Stoned.
He had prayed
For rain.
They paid
And stoned
When rain stayed
Distant.
Our earth God's promise
Never to deluge,
But will rain
Ever rain again?

At last
One night
The cycle turns.
Heavenly drops
Pound the welcoming earth.
Dawn wakens
Surveys the land
Vibrant with winged ants.
Doves and ibis feast.
Strong earth-linked folk
Wield joyous hoes,
And in their eyes
Float visions of new crops,
Bananas, yams, and corn
The invisible cord
Tying Maasai cattle
to the unique water hole
Stretches, lengthens.

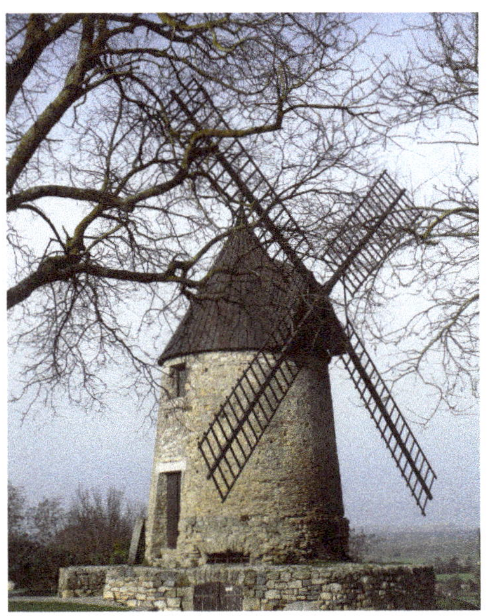

Secure again,
They wander freely.
The herder's smile
Grows wide.
His knobbed stick raised
"We live in cycles,"
He gushes.
"Now there is water
But the dry winds will come."

In a Mirror Darkly

Through a glass darkly I saw
News reports from Rwanda, sites of massacres,
Rows of skulls and once-human bodies
Collapsed like marionettes with broken strings,
Murderers unrepentant and uncowed;
Current events in Burundi
Frame three hundred killed here,
Huddled together in a displaced camp;
Seventy killed there, dispersed
Along the river
In thick banana groves.
The others are the enemy!
Who are these people?
Can you explain genocide?
Population pressures, fear,
Generations of inequity and iniquity,
Manifest destiny, clinging to political power,
and other causes real and invented.
Where is respect of persons?
Where are tolerance, love,
And a cup of cold water?

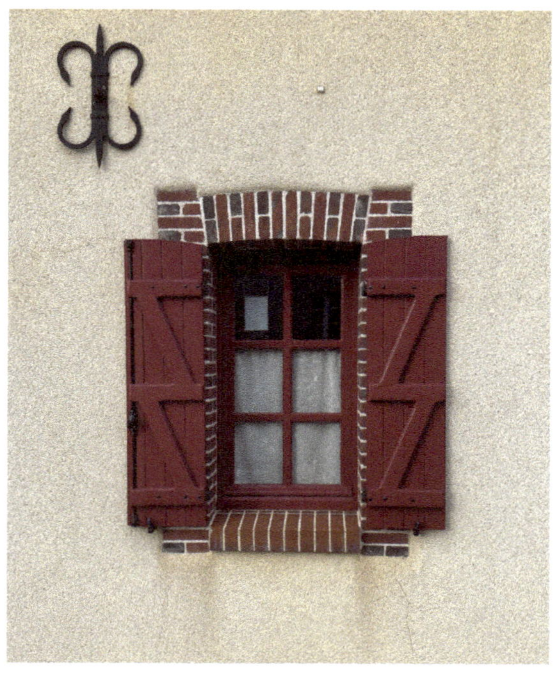

Deep behind that same glass darkly,
Looking again, I glimpsed confusedly:
Not the proud tall Tutsi
Favored by the colonial powers
and trained to lead
But cut down in his prime;
Not the strong, hardworking Hutu
Raising his head to realize his potential,
But scattered over the hills;
Perhaps it was men and women stumbling
Along the Trail of Tears
With memories of green fertile coves
In the Smokey Mountains,
Puzzled by arbitrary decisions
Of another ethnic group.

Perhaps braves scalping a cowering family
In Kentucky because their skins are pale,
And they must be dangerous.
Or perhaps a camp along the Little Bighorn
As women and children in winter
Huddle under worn buffalo robes
And eyes wide
Face in disbelief a cavalry attack?
Who are these people?

Through a glass darkly
Protected by the smokey veil
of denial and self-righteousness?
Or into a glass backed with silver
Where, unprotected, face to face
In the glare of the reflected light,
I see deep within myself
And shrink from the brother within.
From my own hidden darkness
My own potential for destruction
My own complicity.

Who are these people?
What is humanity?
And who am I?

Now, face to face,
I recognize with horror
The humanity I share.

Storm above Lake Tanganyika

The moon has gone
High above Lake Tanganyika
Grumbles the coming storm
Lightening flashes
Behind dark creeping clouds
Nyangoma's men also grumble
Perched high on belvederes
Hidden in banana groves
Mortars aimed at power
In the midnight city
The curfew bars the doors
No cars roll through the streets
Except for unvanquished
Whose curfew holds doors open
The sleeping dream of fertile fields
Of mammoth pots of banana beer
And dowry ceremonies uniting families
Of lyre-horned cattle and egrets
Perched on rounded backs
Of bean pods heavy
And yams thick as your calf
Of rock-strewn crystal streams
Unfilled with hillside mud
Of stately women with plaited hair
Draped in color and grace
Of sturdy men with strong backs
And tireless hoes, with quick smiles
And deep pools of wisdom
Of Abapfasoni and Abashingantahe
Noble women and upright men
Whose voice rings rich with proverb
As dreaming sleep, as sleeping dream
The storm sweeps in
Thunder roll
Mortar crash
Grenade burst
Sleep a memory
The wakened wait in anguish

Which neighbor writhes in pain?
Which neighbor's arm tossed
The pomegranate in its menacing arch?
Which neighbor's heart weeps for her child
Calling for comfort?

And as the rain drums
As courage melts
And all hearts quiver
A minaret springs to life
"Allah u Akbar"
The dark, the storm, and hate disband
Dawn must be near at hand.

Year One

One year ago in August last
we stood before the registrar,
our signatures the decade guarantee,
then only dreaming of Colorado mountains
and the Arkansas River.
This year your sparkling eyes
match the pale blue Colorado sky
and the corresponding azure lake.
Those eyes, ever alert,
spot nature's beauties,
tiny pikas in rocks,
hawks circling above quaking aspens,
crimson gilia, and Indian paintbrushes
against blue spruce background.
Strong legs push up rocky slopes
and through flower-strewn meadows.
"Gorgeous," you repeat,
happily sharing the wonder
and a warm embrace
with grateful partner.
Year one of union,
full of adventure,
full of delight,
the first of ten.

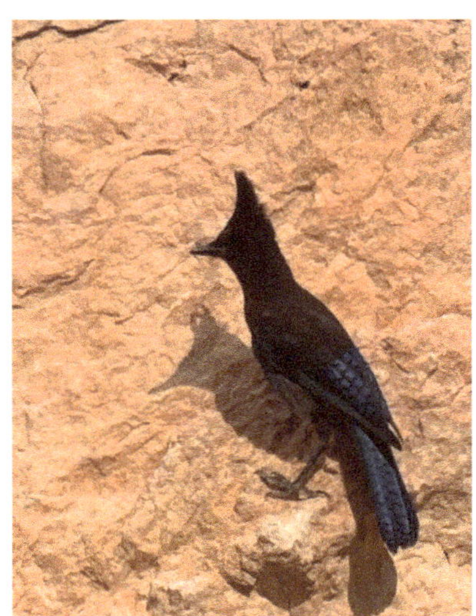

Four Score and More
(for Sydney)

Lover of nature, lover of beauty,
and lover
Walking queen-like
down mountain paths
eyes ever alert for color and form
of glorious blossoms
and heart-shaped rocks
Miles driven with loved ones
through the seasons of life
Mellowed and sharpened
by four-score years of joys and pains
but reveling in the moment
sharing sparkle in eye
and enticing smile
Loving the rustling leaves
atune to the rippling water
cascading over mossy rocks
Ever grateful for forest quiet
and nature's peace
Welcoming supporting hands
and always a partner's touch
celebrating eighty years
of curiosity and creativity
Lover of beauty, lover of nature,
and lover.

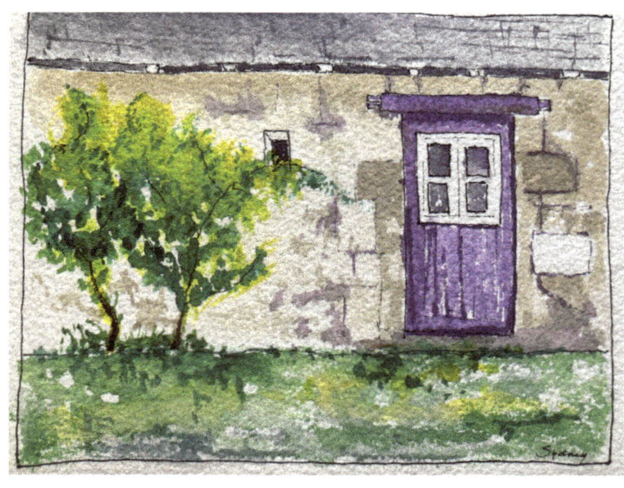

Winter Solstice

It's the mid-December solstice,
so today the sun stood still,
hanging low in the southern sky.
Darkness came early,
but come walk with me,
and let us be alert to the sounds of night,
the wind in bare oak branches,
the plaintive call of the screech owl
and even the soft flutter of his silent wings
in the great stillness of this darkling world.
Extinguish the torch.
Let eyes dilate to capture
hidden mysteries of shape and form
and follow scudding clouds in moonless sky.
Light can dazzle,
and the sun will surely rise again,
but let us revel in this darkness
that brings such restful comfort.
Clothed in shades of black,
hand in mittened hand,
we melt into deep shadows,
welcomed as denizens of this winter's night.
We delve into our inner darkness,
sloughing off all weighty thoughts
of greed and vengeance,
finding calm and deep repose,
knowing that this longest, darkest night
announces new beginnings.

A Birthday Palette

In this ode to colors,
when the Carolina sky above our misty mountains
mirrors the morning blue in your twinkling eyes,
I see you as Vermeer's Girl with the Pearl Earring
and her wide blue scarf
and think of peasants in Southern France
harvesting dyer's woad from rolling hills,
extracting from its desiccated leaves,
after soaking and fermenting,
those marvelous shades of blue,
a source of peace and wealth.

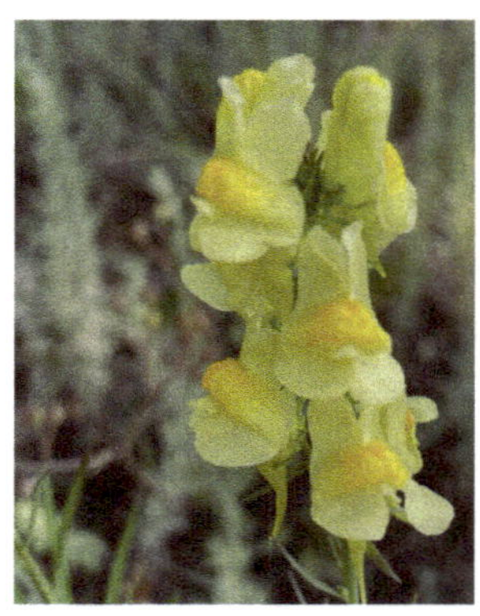

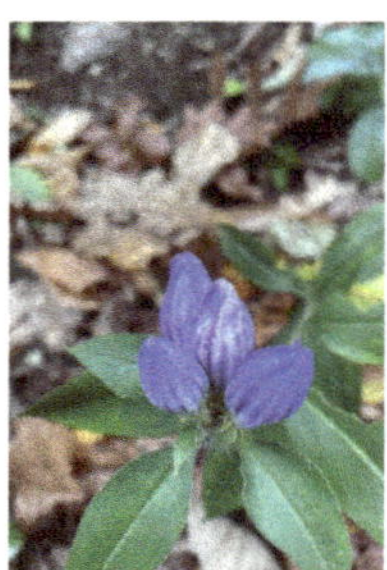

In your palette gold sparkles too,
and yellows—sunflowers in Colorado
and along narrow roads in France,
bowing low as racing cyclists sweep by,
like murmurating starlings,
their multi-colored jerseys
flashing in the sun,
plump lemons squeezed to mix with amber tea,
citrine cloud linings on early morning walks,
the glow of royal saffron,
giving color to curative paellas.

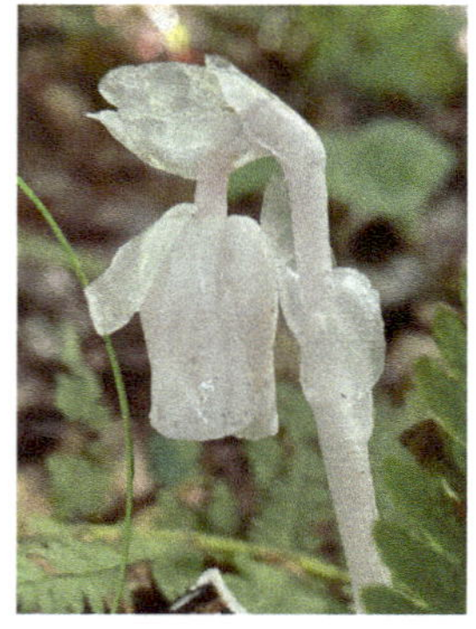

Pale colors too attract your eye:
Blanquette de Limoux
bubbling like champagne in your birthday glass,
and along rushing mountain streams
on twisting, shapely trunks,
a canopy of sourwood blossoms
against green leafy background,
nectar magnets for honeybees
and the golden sweetness they create.

The burnt siena of Utah hoodoos,
the ochres in our Piedmont clay,
and granite grays of lichen-covered rocks
along our Carolina trails
are not the tones
that first your brush seeks out
in open palette choices.
But like blues, reds too are irresistible,
the deep dark garnet red
that warms our dwelling wall,
symbol of love and friendship;
the rich burgundy of my cabernet
standing strong beside your pale pinot,

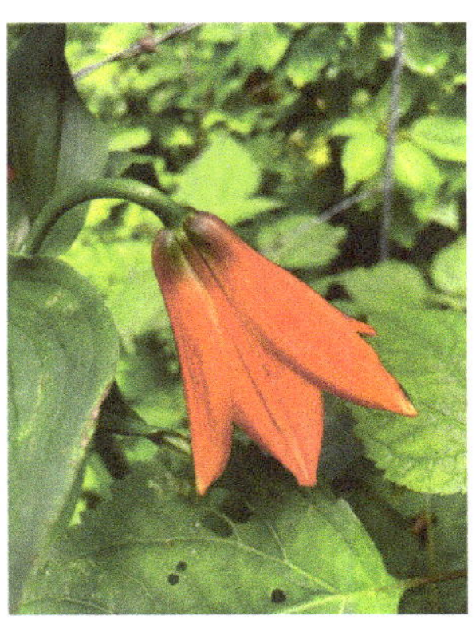

the cardinal in his priestly robe
calling "cheer, cheer, cheer,"
fire pinks bright red on slate gray granite cliffs,
the ruby throat of hummingbirds
that zoom and dart and sip sweet liquid
your hands prepare,
and sunset's vermilion-shaded clouds
o'er Western mountain peaks,
and from your Traverse days
the cerise of summer cherries
in full profusion, hanging thick on trees.

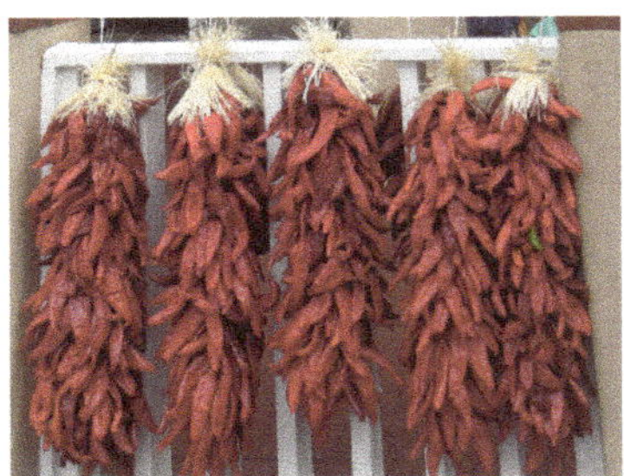

On birthday nights, you long
for moonless skies as black as coal,
when brilliant streaks of flashing meteors
shower above our heads
in heaven's arching dome.
These days, the little black dress
you donned for parties
gives way to charcoal hiking pants
with special pockets holding sustenance and phone.
You resonate of course with every color
green, orange, violet, pink.

But nothing beats the peace,
the confidence of all those blues:
our bluebirds on birdbath,

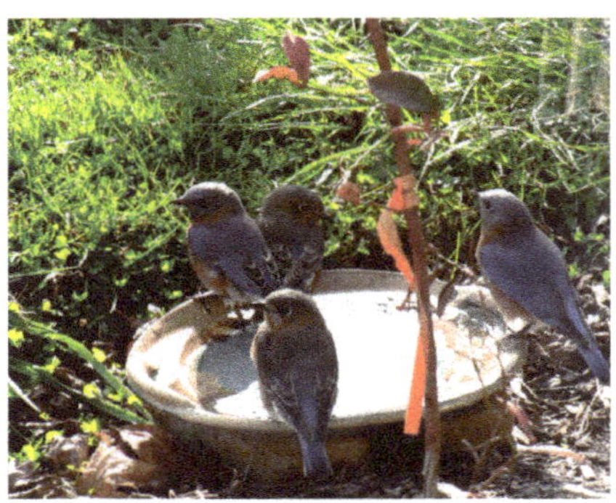

your cerulean hiking shirt
prepared for Gallic trails,
early morning roadside chicory
caught in camera lens,
blue spruce with pale new growth,
cobalt as you turn on Cobalt Ridge,
in obsidian blue pearl car,
the beauteous hues on fabrics
rough, smooth, denim, silk,
of woad and indigo,
and stains on fingers from blueberries
saved from dark gray catbird,
their deep blue melted sweetness
resting hot 'neath crispy topping.
All these blues and more
reflect forever
in your sparkling eyes,
with peace, confidence, and especially love.

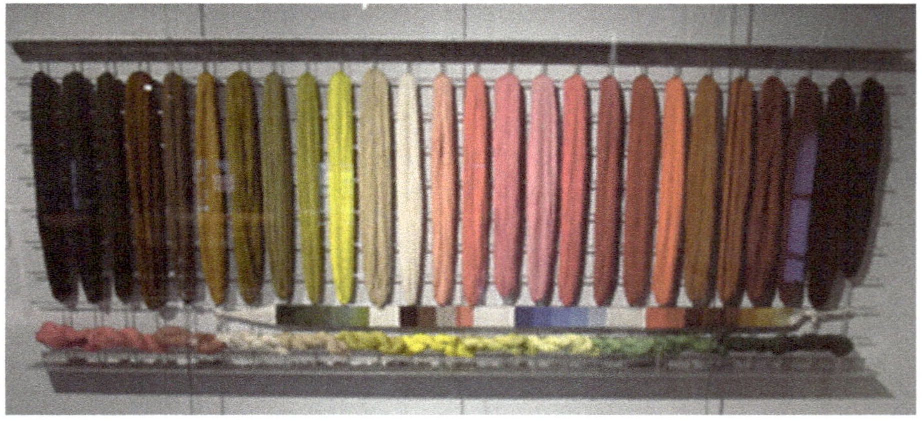

Winter Night

The winter night is dark on mountain crest,
the moon a tiny crescent in the west.
A chill wind howls through frozen air,
pine branches thrashing in despair.

The news tonight is of darkest hour,
of wars, of greed and thirst for power,
of hate for differences and others,
not recognizing that all are brothers.

The leaves have fallen and the grass is brown.
the season's news drags courage down.
We know our friends face illnesses and sorrows,
we hear of distant massacres and horrors.

We grieve for goals we have not met
and ache for acts that we regret.
We mourn the loss of those so dear,
who once so vibrant brought us cheer.

So one tall candle let us light,
find comfort in its glow so bright,
lift mugs of cider mulled with spice
to counteract the winter's ice.

Do whisper love's sweet soothing tones
to warm my sinews and my bpnes,
and grace me with your soft caress,
dispelling anxiousness and stress.

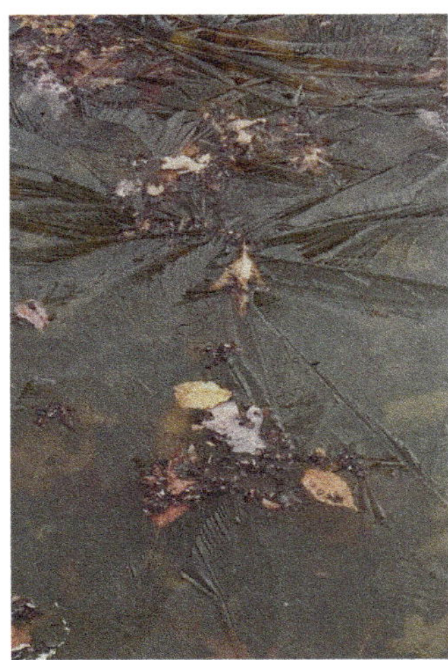

81

Companion in Winter

Stepping in from walk in icy woods
with cashmere scarf still gracing neck,
Stay near, companion of my winter nights.
Sit near this fire that warms our hearts
and keeps at bay fierce frigid gusts.

Turn on colored Christmas lights
to chase gray thoughts.
Speak to me softly of years gone by,
giving voice to shapes and colors,
creative dreams that found their form
through twinkling eyes and nimble hands.

During springtime's fresh young years
we wandered continents apart,
savoring nectar from other flowers
caressed by soft sweet vernal breezes.

We welcomed life's long summer days
shared in different lands,
sporting lithe tanned bodies on strands of sand
and watching children grow and learn,
smithing silver, or speaking foreign tongues.

And then, at summer's end,
we watched as one life's chapter closed.
We clung to savored memories,
but autumn wine we drank alone
and faced a future void of joy.

But now, in the winter of our lives,
loneliness has fled, and joy returns.
The days are short and nights are long.
Do light the candle so that I may see
the facial lines that pain and smiles have carved.

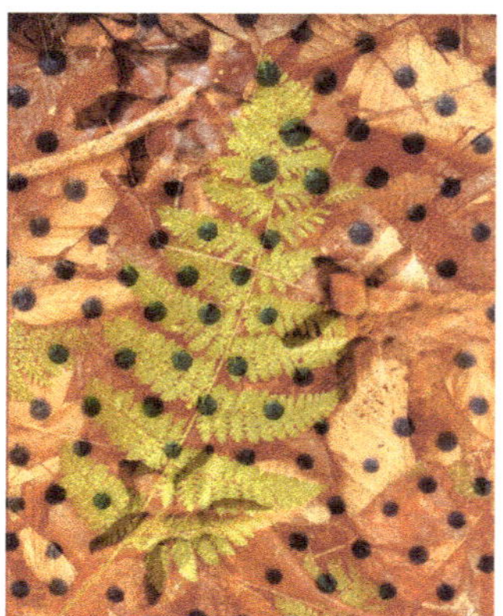

Turn your eyes to me
that I might feel with you those stabs of pain
from spring and summer past.
And let me always share alike
with whispered syllables
those deep sweet memories that warm your heart.

Stay close, companion of my winter life.
Give me your hand.
Together let us watch the fire burn low
and keep our sacred vigil
until the last red glow expires.

Pelican Diving

Brown pelican skims the waves,
wing tips lightly brushing surface.
He rises up, eyes trained below,
then reefs both wings
and dives to capture prey.
Sometimes he reaches target,
sometimes he comes up empty.
As pelican knows the winds
and reads the ocean swells
to grow and thrive
and never fails
to rise again when plunge is fruitless,
may we as well
chart path and goals,
greet welcome joys and sweet success,
and slough off life's reverses.

Commitment

If like Daniel Defoe in his plague year journal,
we kept a journal of this viral year,
along with isolation and fears
that keep us up at night
thinking of loved friends and family
and praying they maintain health and courage,
we could also marvel at our growing sense
of mutual care and joy together.

Both our spirits have been nurtured
in mountain highs and valley lows
in the purple mountains of Virginia
and the russet, golden slopes of Colorado.
We both find peace in winding trails,
pausing in wonder
at a splashing brook,
the song of the wood thrush,
or the delicate beauty of a cranefly orchid.

We both remember deep past loves
that have made us what we are,
and we know what soulmates mean.
With gratitude and joy,
we celebrate discovery in our Carolina mountains
of newfound artistry and harmony
from deep within our souls.

We know that time is fleeting,
and hence we want our friends
to know that we commit
for the days we have left on this earth,
with the help of our friends and the Divine,
to share our lives—our dreams and sorrows,
our aspirations and our love.

We shall aim to live simply on our Mother Earth,
seeking sustainability, conserving resources,
alert to the beauty of floral color,
like the trout lily and Oconee Bells in spring,
and to the melodious birdsong
and leaf-scratching antics of towhee and thrasher.

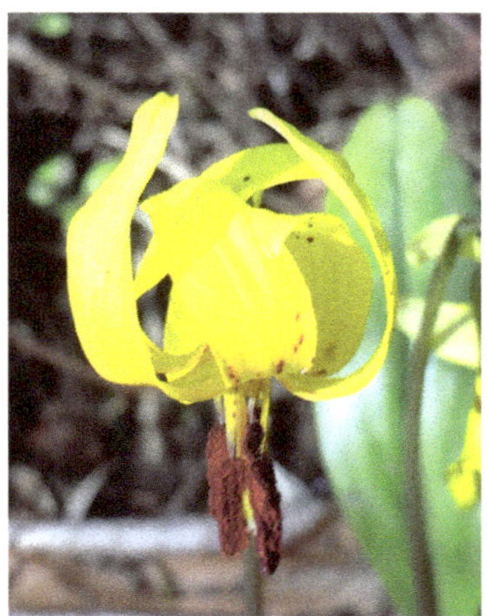 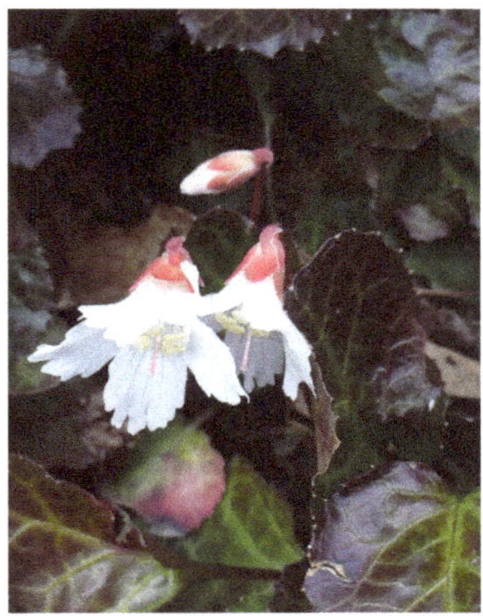

We shall strive to remember
to join in joyful service to community,
to share resources with those in need,
and, when possible,
to encourage smiles on faces
and peace in hearts.

We shall remind each other
to develop our talents,
to uplift and nurture, seeking justice,
to practice small acts of kindness,
to make life richer, to walk humbly,
and to seek to fill our days with meaning
as long as we both shall live.

Darkness

As night falls over the mountains,
the last glimmer fading in the west,
may we welcome the darkness
and celebrate the peace it brings.

Even as the shortest day draws near,
the day has been long,
though scarcely long enough
to finish all our mundane tasks.

The sparkling little lights on Christmas trees
don't try to mimic daylight
but add depth to darkness,
their colors adding life to black beyond.

Listen to the rustle of wind in bare branches,
to the lonesome call of the owl
poised to fly noiselessly between spreading oaks,
its ears attuned to scurrying feet.

Watch above the eastern hills,
Orion once more rising bravely
into near-winter sky,
followed by his faithful dog.
Revel on this moonless night
with bluish streaks of shooting stars,
Geminid reminders of our infinite space
and of wondrous creativity.

And as we sit beneath bright constellations,
dark silhouettes framed against starry sky,
you touch my hand and whisper
words of peace and comfort.

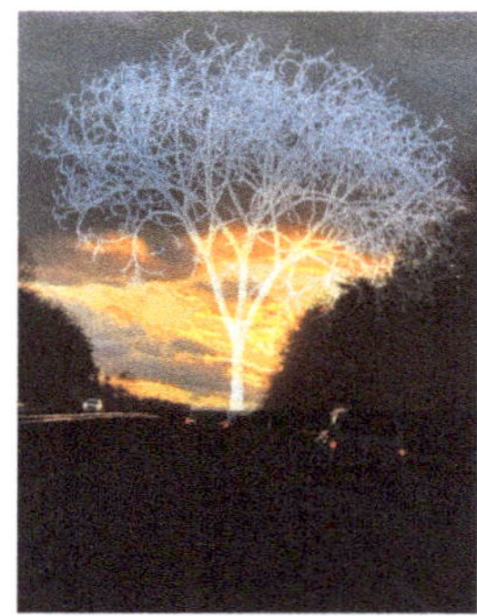

Fleeting

Clouds drift slowly overhead,
leaving under summer sun just shadows
that themselves last no more than dreams
flitting away when sleep departs.

The train passes, its whistle blasting
across the valley, vibration humming
on silvery track, and then it's gone,
even echos fading in the night.

Water droplets in the mountain stream
carry with them springtime petals,
together flowing onward toward the Gulf,
unnoticed by high up peaks.

Over years across earth's surface,
what trace have your own footsteps left
on tropical red laterite
or black sand beaches?

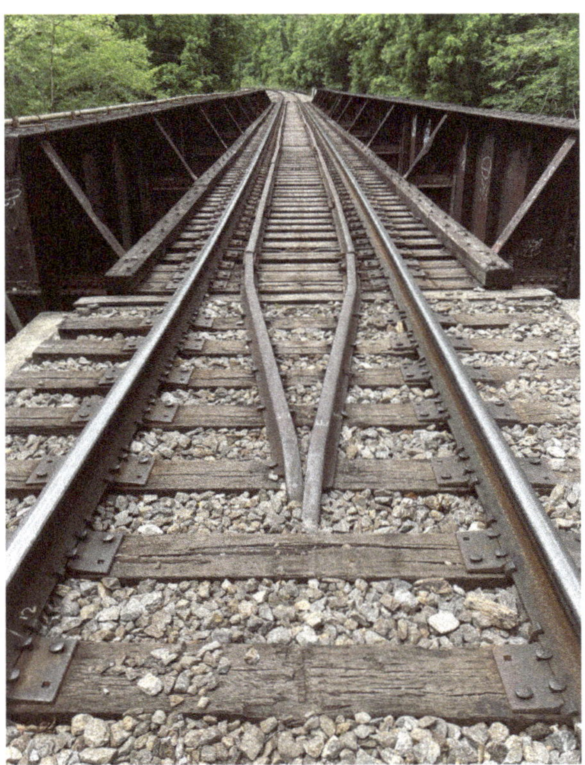

13th of Thermidor

In Thermidor, that month of warmth,
the fierce west wind
swept o'er Wyoming plains,
chasing tumbleweeds before it
and scattering the clouds.

As Perseus climbed high in the east
and the wind whistled through the prairie grass,
streaks of light filling moonless sky
in their annual display of joy,
a new life awoke and drew first breath.

In the tale of newborn princess
there came some fairies,
who bequeathed their gifts,
wealth and beauty,
skill, grace and fame.

In this Wyoming tale
the heat of summer
brought to this new babe
the germ of human warmth,
expressed in love
for friend, consort, and family.

The brisk west wind
brought strength and curiosity,
the wish to roam, to wander,
to find adventure,
to seek new states.

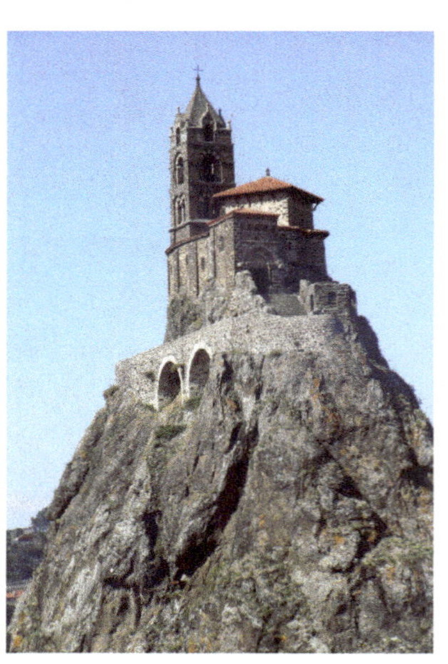

And the faithful Perseids,
streaking 'cross the sky,
brought her light and inspiration,
the drive to find new forms
and fill the world
with shapes and colors.

Today in celebrating
four-score years and two,
far from wind-swept bronze Wyoming hills
now 'neath soft green Appalachian peaks
as Thermidorian heat
each year warms heart and soul,
as breeze inspires,
as shooting stars
careen and dance above
again this year, that life stays new,
creating beauty,
spreading joy,
and sharing love.

The She-Wolf

Sleep-walking through life,
As on a winding mountain path
Under low grey skies by day,
Bare beech winter branches pasted
Dark against the gloomy clouds,
I mourned my best years gone.

As darkness fell on twisted laurel arms,
From 'neath the everlasting green
Of waxy rhododendron leaves
Peered out the blue-green eyes
Of a solitary she-wolf, tall and strong!

The deep eyes smiled encouragement,
And in their glow I saw on bare beech branches
Swelling buds announcing new spring life.
Reflected in their light, I saw
The zephyr wind unwrapping low dark clouds,
Gifting rising moon and joys serene!

Winter Delight

The trees are bare and the grass is dead,
the days are short and the cold wind grips,
but look! winterberry fruit now glows red,
and trees begin to show their swollen tips.

In this time of year with longest nights
and chilly winds that take their toll,
may we stay alert to small delights
that captivate and warm our soul.

The pale half moon hangs high above the hills,
in morning sun a bluebird dozes,
camellia blossoms display their frills,
a flock of robins in our maple poses.

A ring-necked duck paddles round in pond,
we watch the geese in tight formation rise
toward azure blue of valley skies beyond
and crimson clouds that sunset dyes.

Sniff welcome smells of frying bacon,
of freshly ground dark-roasted coffee,
to frosty scents of white-oak smoke awaken
and relish taste of homemade toffee.

Woodpeckers' drumming fills the air
and church bells all their songs employ.
A screech owl calls his partner fair,
the cheery wren sings out her joy.

At each moment when we note delight,
self-pity flees and peace arises.
So let us keep our senses bright
to savor winter's small surprises.

A January Blessing

When news reports of hate and lies
this week join January's arctic gales,
may you draw delight in observation
as day by day the sun's path rises in the south,
adding increments of time to daylight hours,
and may you feel that light arising in your heart.

When like avalanche on snowy slopes
or floods on mountain streams,
the crushing thoughts of loss and grief
conspire to overwash your soul,
may you cling to solid memories,
like river rocks, so firm and sound,
of joyous moments shared.

When the trees stand bare of leaves
and the fields stay brown,
may you sense the force of hidden roots
stretching irrepressibly toward fertile soil
and note that hope for growth to come
lies waiting in the swelling maple buds.

When painful moments try your soul
and you think you face the world alone,
remember that good friends reach out
with songs and smiles and warm embrace,
and may you pay that back in kind
and know that love when shared is gold.

So when the harsh north wind whistles
through your cap and scarf
to chill your bones and mind,
may you warm a cup of chocolate
and simply sit with those you love
by candlelight or flickering open fire.

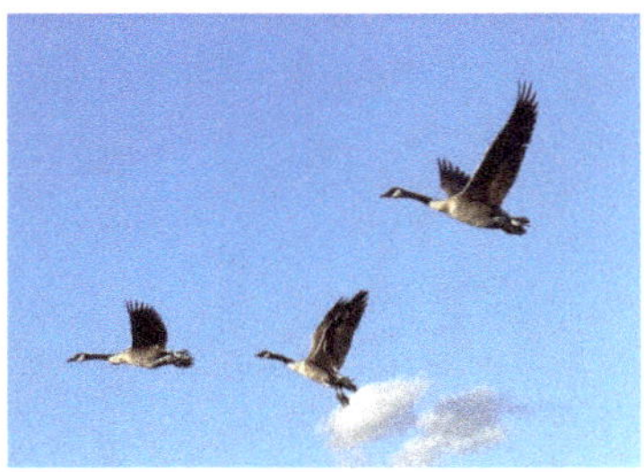

Tom's Drone

I'm a drone, not the useless
male honeybee that stays near the ground.
But new and bright, battery charged, my vision triggered,
I'm sent by handler high into the sky
to get a bird's eye view of life
in our home's peaceful valley.

Soaring just below the clouds,
I look down on the river snaking to the west,
and I see the glades where ancient Cherokees
set summer camps for game and fish,
oblivious to the coming immigrant wave
that would wash them from their homes.
Was our valley always peaceful?

I see the pass between peaks
where those early settlers rode
on twisting paths, curious
as they started down
through chestnut-strewn forest floor,
greedy to find new land
and steal from those who lived there.

I swoop low over a reservoir
and, through the clear waters,
wonder at old barns and cabins framed beneath
and picture residents removed
from valley fields, their land taken
by eminent domain to water
seeds of progress for the city.

I dip and bank above two metal tracks,
rising parallel up mountain grade
above tunnels blasted through high ridges,
and still smell the smoke of old steam engines
twisting serpentine paths past mounds
of convict graves, price paid by black and white,
so trade could grow and thrive.

As battery weakens and handler
calls me back to peaceful valley home,
I gladly wipe from memory
those painful scenes from by-gone days,
and my camera-eye now closed,
I fail to see those who suffer now,
the homeless, and the lonely.

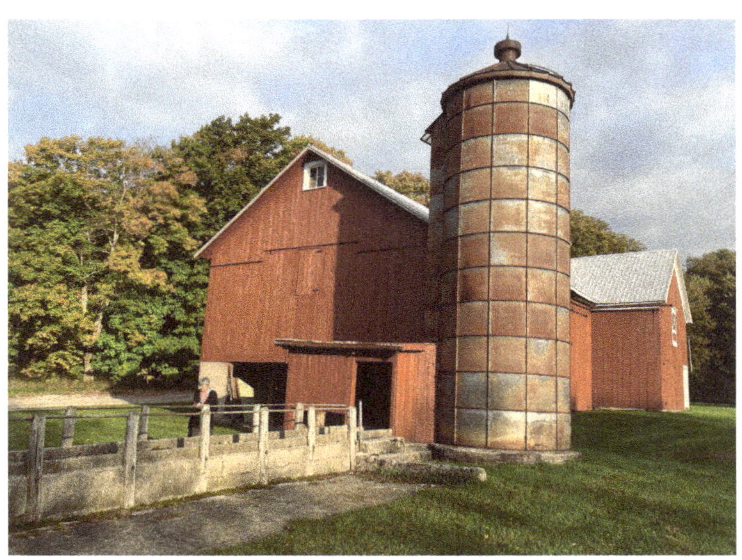

Juneteenth

The days get longer.
Backs bent, heavy hoes in hand,
we stretch across the field
from dawn to dusk,
chopping weeds
from cotton rows.

It's near midsummer
and to celebrate the longest day
we'll jump through flames
to chase away those evil thoughts
that never will we see our homeland
except when life has passed
and we again traverse the great salt sea.

Then from the town
on this June Nineteenth
arise strong cheers and cries.
And quickly the word is passed,
flying on strong feathered wings:
"We're truly free!
No more are families split
and sold like cows and goats."

These hoes now belong to us,
and we raise them high
like banners in the sky.
Our fetters gone,
we belong once more,
belong only to ourselves.

Midsummer

The earth keeps turning,
and days have slowly lengthened.
Bluebirds begin early serenades,
welcoming midsummer,
and thieving catbirds stay alert
in blueberry patch as dusks linger late.

The rains of April, warmth of May,
have given life to fertile ground,
and early summer's grass is lush,
and trees spread bright green canopies,
nature's rich abundance
in preparation for changing seasons,
for shorter days
and lengthening nights.

So too at this midsummer
we celebrate our health,
the fire of joy
and life's rich fullness,
but turn our thoughts as well,
as daylight begins contracting,
to shortening strides,
to sweetening songs,
and calming spirits
in harmony with sun's southward turn.

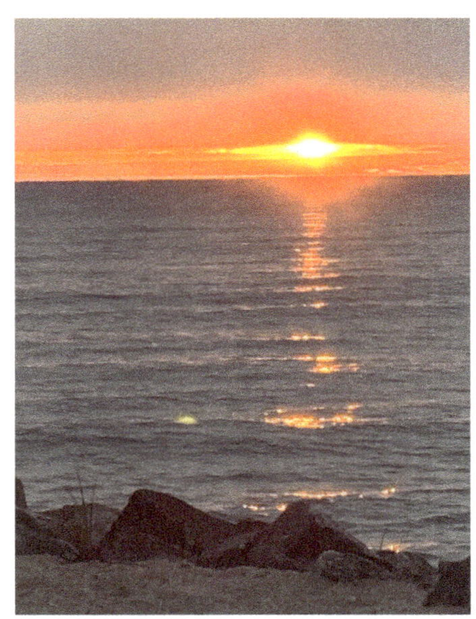

Green Mountains at Season's End
(upon the loss of my daughter)

I live beneath green mountain peaks
graced by soaring hawks,
red shoulders caught in morning light,
calling to their young,
demonstrating lofty flight,
and watching, tear in eye,
as strong offspring
disappear over hemlock ridge.

In our protected valley
darting hummingbirds swoop and dive,
making final visits
to pink phlox, yellow dahlias,
and bright cardinal flowers
before leaving this land
for parts unknown.

Our summer's gone.
Black gum leaves on mountain slopes
turn brilliant red,
the first to show
the season's end.
The sourwood seeds,
dried muscadines,
and black wild cherry fruit
drop to the ground,
their role of nourishing
both bird and bee
now finished.

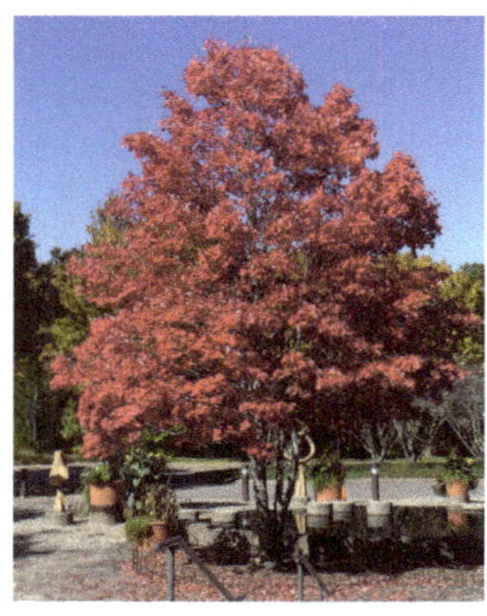

Colors paint our evening clouds,
and August's early sunsets
mark the end of youthful life,
of melodies, of joyful smiles,
of summer showers,
of growth, of new adventure.

But 'neath eternal mountains green,
of moments shared
on winding trails,
of joyous exclamation
at budding flower,
and hawk's shrill call
at butterfly's return
and sweet bird song,
eternal memories abound.

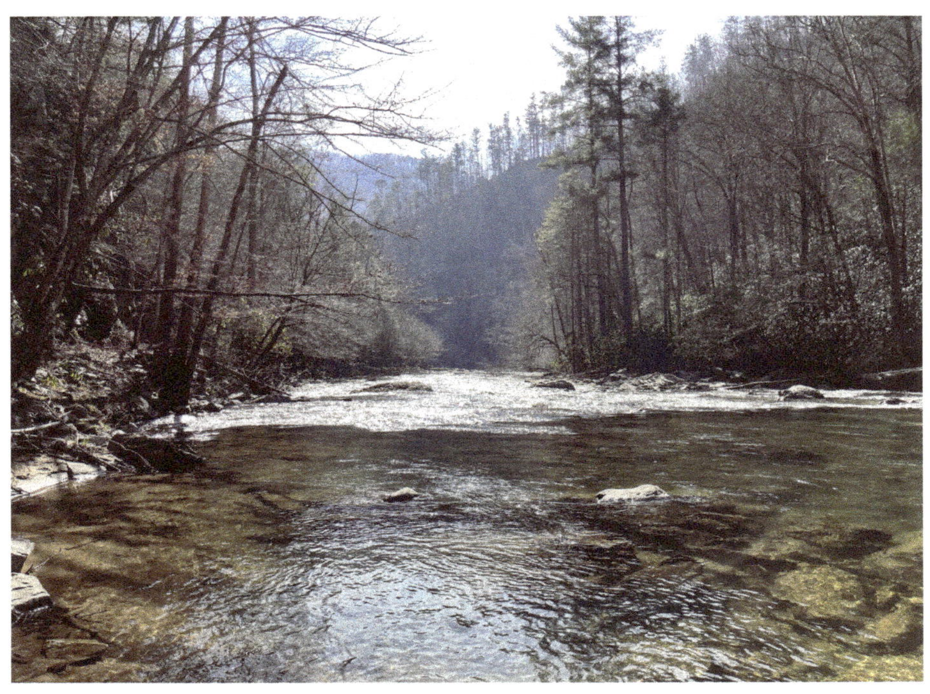

Catbird Thief

Grey catbird watches from yonder post,
meows twice as a warning;
on blueberry bushes
berries begin the pink blush
of rabbiteyes.

Catbird hops to the ground,
sidles up to a bush,
hops to a low branch,
and plucks once more a pinkish fruit,
not waiting for the blue.

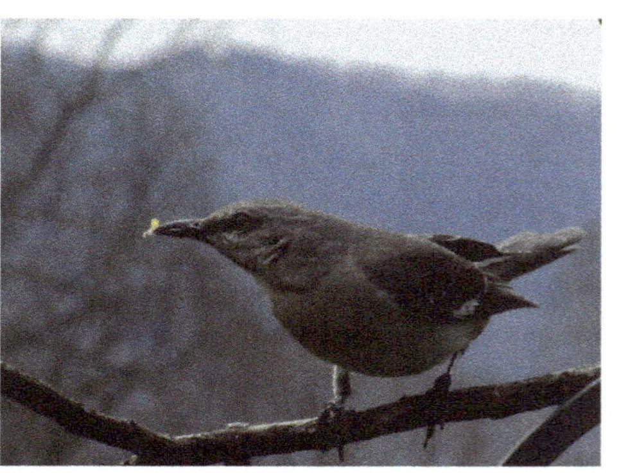

With berry in beak,
flies up to a nearby branch,
winks at me through the window,
raises head,
and berry disappears.

Will my dreams
of blueberry pies evaporate?
Perhaps I should dream
of four and twenty catbirds
baked in a pie.

Tree Swallow

With nimble acrobatics
the tree swallow swoops and dives,
reveling in fluid motion,
gathering insects from pond's surface,
or snatching mosquitoes from thin air.

White breast flashing below,
back glistening iridescent blue
in the morning sun,
he joyfully
fulfills his given task.

A Forest Bath

Come walk with me among tall hemlocks
along this wooded mountain top.
Tread the spongy, soft green moss
and place your hand on corrugated bark
to sense the strength of towering trunk
and the rising flow of life beneath.

We leave behind the ringing phone,
the traffic, sirens, shouts.
Now listen to the branches rustle,
caressed by west wind's soothing breath,
and to the junco's chirping tune
to keep you distant from its nest.

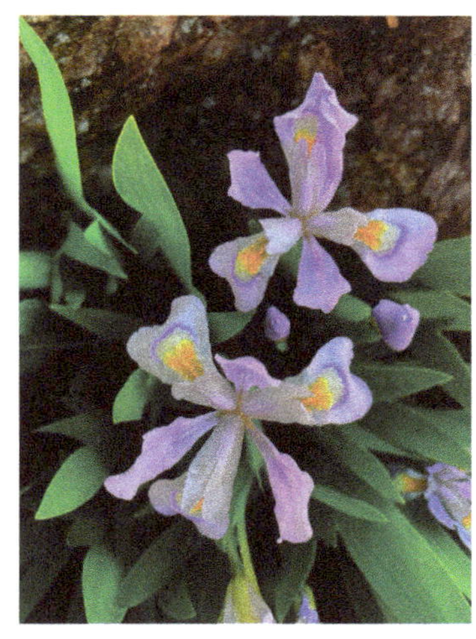

In the silence you will hear
not only murmurs of your beating heart
but whispers of communicating roots
of oaks and beeches, pines, and firs,
passing along their fears, their dreams,
and bidding welcome to our presence there.

Breathe in the acrid scent of heart-shaped
Galax leaf and rhododendron flowers'
heady, captivating clove perfume
dispelling haze of asphalt, smoke, and gasoline
that clog the soul and dull the mind
from city streets now left behind.

Our eyes take in the varied tones of green,
the Carolina blue between the lofty boughs,
the dappled sun in shadows on the ground,
the red and black of cardinal and flicker,
huckleberries ripening pink,
an artist's palette laid out for inspiration.

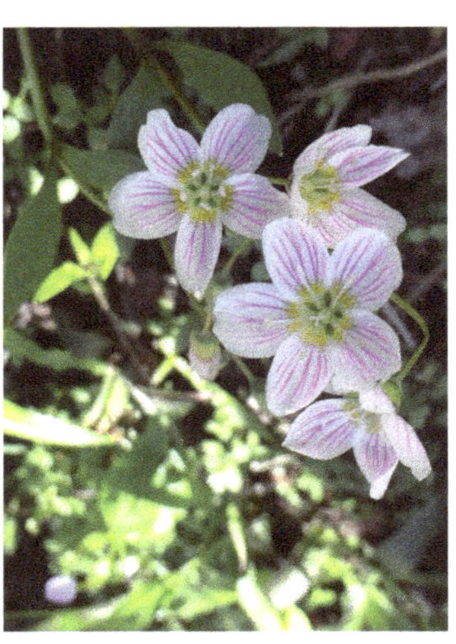

The soft green moss mid hemlocks tall
with branches singing in the wind
harmonize with thought and limb.
Sweet aromas and joyous colors
wash fatigue and sorrows from our skin
and leave us cleansed in mind and soul.

Canal du Midi

From Toulouse to the sea
the sleek canal winds through the plains,
fed by water from black mountains.
Your serpentine path,
laid out three centuries ago
by level, rod, and measuring wheel,
now lined with stately sycamores,
with pick and shovel was carved in beauty.

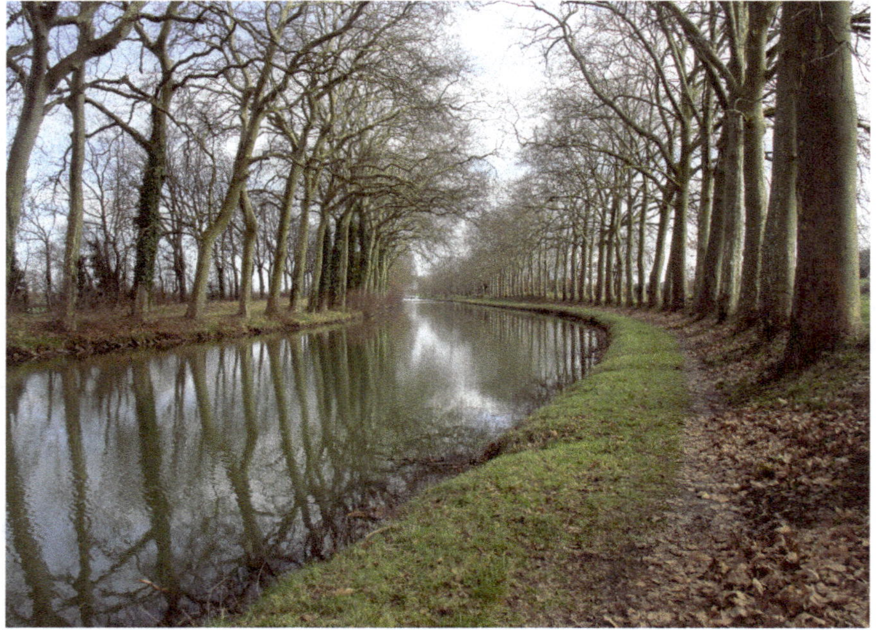

The water from the mountain springs
now lifts, not barges full of wheat or salt
but sturdy tourist river craft
gayly flying flags with fleurs de lys on blue
and bronze Occitan crosses on white.
While seated 'neath those billowing flags,
guests sip wine on foredeck,
feeling the lift as water rises in the lock,
waving to the lock tender standing at his post.

To right and left stretch fields of Sunflowers,
heads heavy with seeds hanging
from tall stalks, brown and gold
against evergreen oaks.

Through courtyard gates
pastel blue fabric hangs drying in the sun,
dyed deep with woad,
and in the distance
outlined on rocky crests
stand broken turrets of ancient castles,
circled by black ravens.

From nearby villages waft
the heady scents of cassoulet, its white beans flavored
with chunks of goose and sausages.
Eyes scan the straight green lines
of manicured vineyards in the plains,
imagining crisp white wine from Piquepoule grapes
and noting heavy grapes on pale limestone hills
awakening dreams of rich red Minervois
from Syrah, Grenache, Mourvèdre.

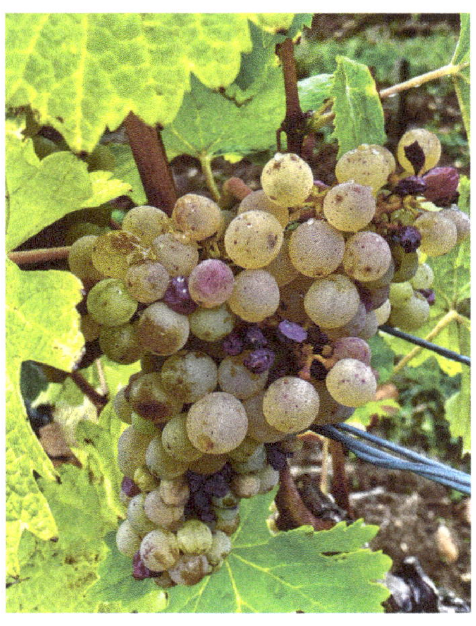

With your sycamore-lined banks
and vineyards on the hills,
with mallards splashing in your dark green water,
may you wind on for centuries to come
under warm meridional sun.

Child's First Library Visit, 1950

Today my six years have turned to seven.
My dad drops me by some beckoning stairs
rising upward toward my childhood heaven,
wide library doors, an answer to prayers.

The woman behind the book-strewn space
greets me with warm and cheerful smile,
knowing from my stride and eager face
that I must be a budding bibliophile.

She guides me through pathways to racks
of large tomes filled with strange creatures,
books with mysterious numbers and colorful backs,
shows me fish that climb and other weird features.

She awakens dreams of wondrous lands,
of mountain rivers and piedmont creeks,
of wind-blown undulating Saharan sands,
of soaring, snowy Himalayan peaks.

She leads me through some culinary sections,
promoting purple Okinawan sweet potatoes,
finds Chinese, Greek, and African confections
and Italian golden apples (or tomatoes.)

But then she halts by books with darker tones,
with splintered backs and wrinkled pages,
tales of massacres and piles of bones,
land grabs, greed throughout the ages.

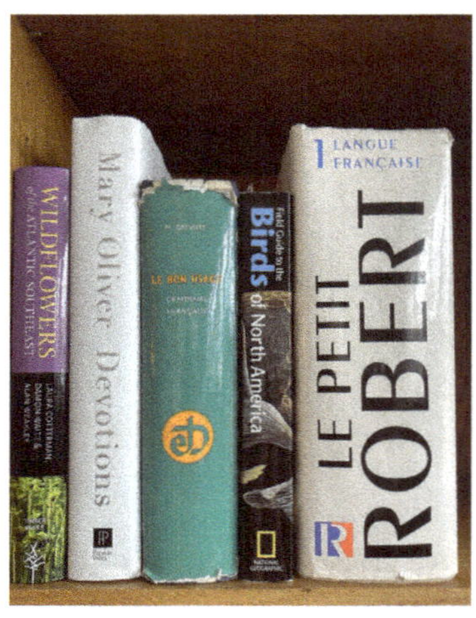

She says "a little learning is a dangerous thing,"
and points to fountains marked "colored" and "white":
"not everyone can taste the crystal spring,
while segregation is still our plight."

"Yes, we have those who preach separation.
But as you exit these halls you must also reflect
that in books we can gather true inspiration
and models for lives based on respect."

Voices on the River I

The morning fog
shrouds late summer river,
caressing the valley with cottony palms.
In the distance,
voices rise up to us,
muffled but cheery.
Soon,
pulled along by relentless current,
like inexorable fate,
water fed by mountain springs
in constant journey toward the Gulf,
kayaks, blue, red, and yellow,
one paddle slapping surface
like beaver's tail,
emerge out past the sourwood tree,
its leaves hinting first red
at summer's end.
Then,
like hummingbirds past window frame,
the colors disappear
beneath black walnut trees,
beyond the foaming rapids.

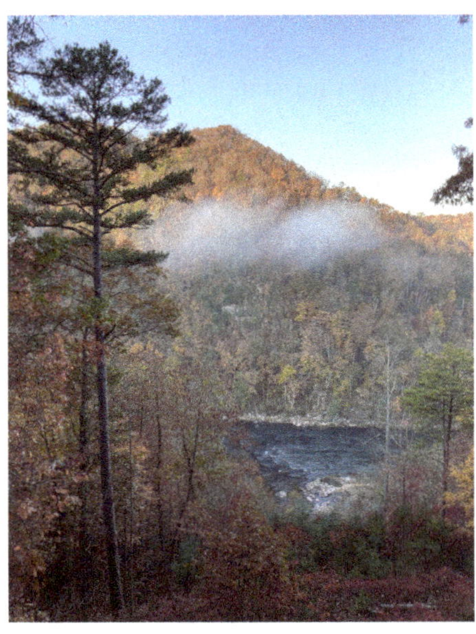

Voices on the River II

Dreaming far above
the French Broad's waters
rushing over rounded rocks,
I hear faint voices from the past.

One young male voice,
alerting friends to progress
with the silky "hoot, hoot"
of Great Horned Owl.
Through the gauze of passing years
I glimpse bronze sinewy shoulders
powering rapid paddle strokes,
propelling venison-laden craft
toward bride and home.

I dream again,
a cacophony of sounds,
the drovers' shouts and curses
in Scottish brogues,
their hickory staves
herding squealing swine
or gobbling fowl
toward piedmont lands
through narrow rocky paths
by water's edge,
panting men and beasts
eager for rest and food
on sandy bottom land
as shadows lengthen.

On rounded river rocks
I hear a clatter,
the hooves of elk
that once roamed these mountain valleys
as stately stag-led harem
from hemlock forest
to grassy farside bank.
From time to time,
his throaty bugle blast,
warning rivals to stay clear.

And through it all,
this ancient river,
though permanent,
is ever changing.
From birth in limpid gurgling springs
to dissolution in the briny deep.
Sometimes clear and peaceful,
reflecting warmth of summer sun,
and sometimes swollen
with treacherous greed,
ripping trees and boulders from banks
when Gulf hurricanes
return deluge to its source.

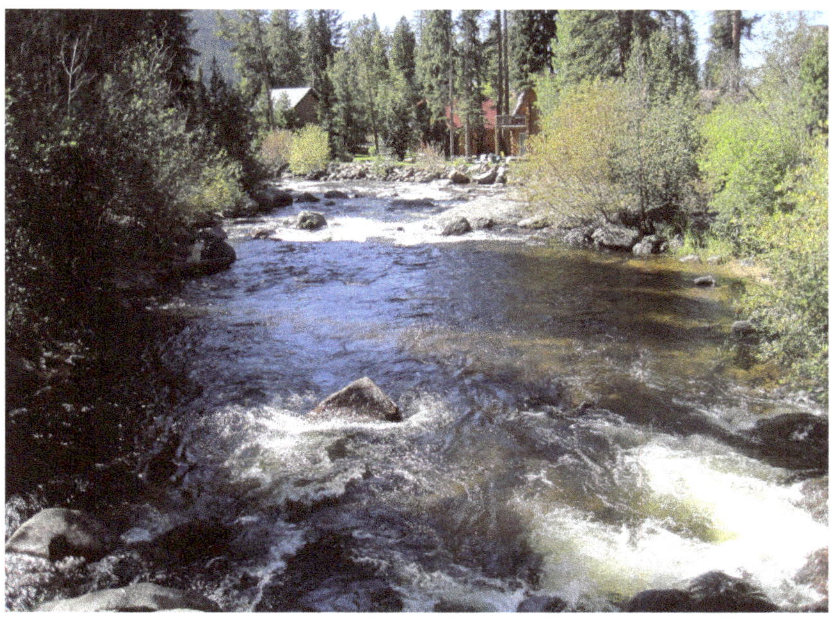

Our lives share river's
mutability,
if not its permanence.
But may our voices too,
in righteous anger or peaceful calm,
communicate to later dreamers
a sense of history
and nature's beauty.

105

L'homme au Lavoir

On the weather-beaten bench
Beside the gently flowing Morin,
A picnic is spread out:
White baguette with yellow Cantal,
Quarters of ripe tomatoes,
Grated carrots bright orange;
Mallards diving, tails upright;
On the green mill pond
Swallows, bellies white, skim the water.
At the lavoir, sleeves rolled up,
A man kneels, washing clothes;
Fatigue and concern
Disappear with the current
Through the waving water grasses.
He rises, places his clothes in a pail,
And starts toward home
Downstream long the river,
Thinking of steak,
Fries, and salad.

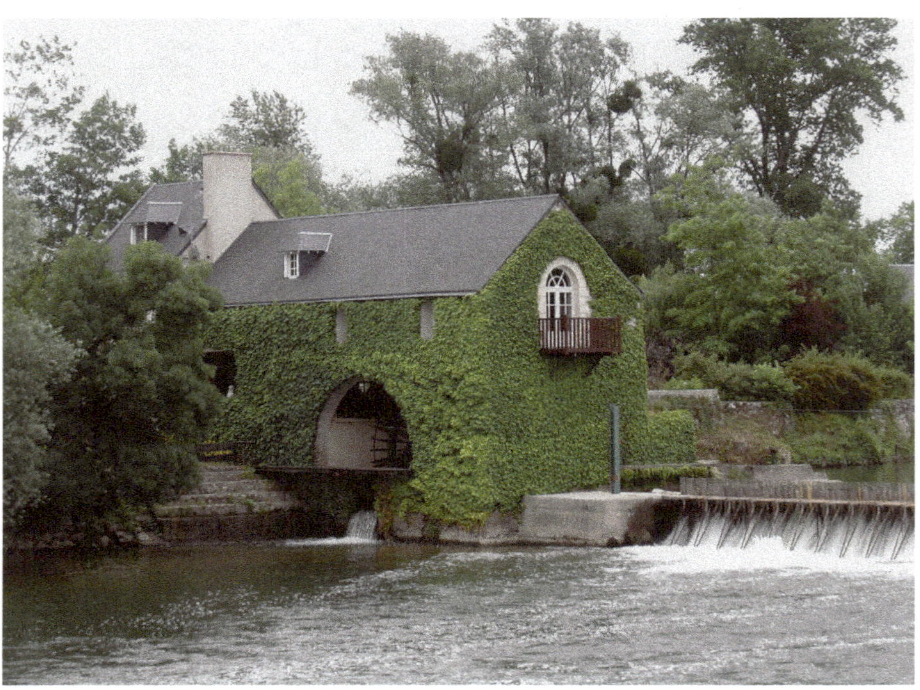

Year Four

"One for the money,
two for the show,
three to make ready
and four to go!"

In three short years
we have explored together
our Carolina trails,
mountains in Utah and Colorado,
lake shore and dunes in Michigan,
beach strands by the ocean,
beautiful French villages,
and tales of sweet memories
from years before.

In this our fourth year,
may we explore new lands
as we walk in stride,
may we surprise each other,
may your eyes continue to sparkle,
may your creative juices flow,
may your touch stay warm,
and may you always sense
my deep abiding wonder
and eternal gratitude
at the sacred love we share.

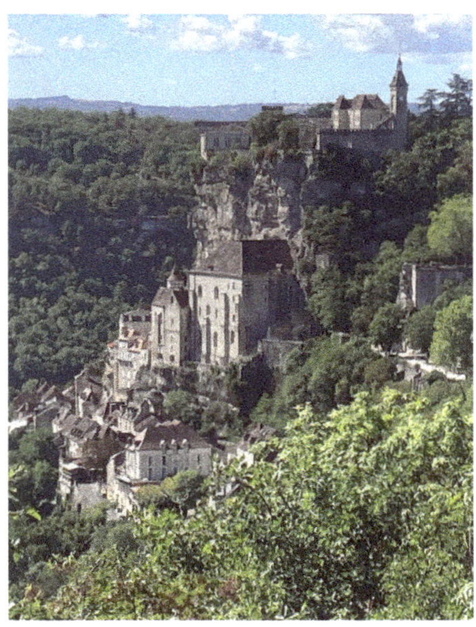

9 798988 176152